D1010585

Blonde Like Me

The Roots of the
Blonde Myth in Our Culture

Natalia Ilyin

A Touchstone Book
Published by Simon & Schuster
New York London Sydney Singapore

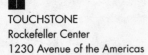

TOUCHSTONE
Rockefeller Center
1230 Avenue of the Americas
New York, NY 10020

Copyright © 2000 by Natalia Ilyin
All rights reserved, including the right of reproduction
in whole or in part in any form.
TOUCHSTONE and colophon are registered
trademarks of Simon & Schuster, Inc.

Designed by Gabriel Levine

Manufactured in the United States of America

10 9 8 7 6 5 4 3 2 1

Library of Congress Cataloging-in-Publication Data
Ilyin, Natalia.
    Blonde like me : the roots of the blonde myth in our culture / Natalia Ilyin.
        p. cm.
    "A Touchstone book."
    1. Blondes. 2. Ilyin, Natalia. 3. United States—Biography. 4. United
States—Social life and customs—20th century. I. Title.
GT6737.I58 2000   99-38960
391.5—dc21   CIP
ISBN 0-684-85214-4

The author and publisher gratefully acknowledge permission to reprint the
following:

Excerpt from *The Moon and the Virgin: Reflections on the Archetypal Feminine*
by Nor Hall. Copyright © 1980 by Eleanor L. Hall. Reprinted by permission of
HarperCollins Publishers.

Excerpts from "The Prophesy of the Seeress" and "The Lay of Rig," translated by
Lee M. Hollander from Edda Saemundar, *The Poetic Edda*, Second Edition,
Revised. Copyright 1962, renewed 1990. Reprinted by permission of the Uni-
versity of Texas Press.

"For Anne Gregory," reprinted with the permission of Simon & Schuster, Inc.
from *The Poems of W. B. Yeats: A New Edition* edited by Richard J. Finneran.
Copyright 1933 by Macmillan Publishing Company; copyright renewed 1961
by Bertha Georgie Yeats.

Acknowledgments

A number of people helped me write this book. My father, Boris Ilyin, read drafts, sent notes, and spent much time hashing out ideas with me over telephone lines. A father like mine is a great gift.

My sister Anna Ilyin McClain, an editor in her own right, worked intensely with me. I could not have written this book without her daily support and kindness. My sisters Nadia Ilyin and Alexandra Ilyin listened to draft after draft of the manuscript and were tirelessly enthusiastic.

Burt Wolf has been a mainstay of encouragement. He introduced me to Cullen Stanley, my literary agent, who gave so much to the project—good sense, laughter, and expertise.

"Compassion" is not a word most people associate with editors. But it is the key to Caroline Sutton, my editor, who had the idea for this book and kept me writing it.

This book grew from my teaching. I owe a great debt to Steve Cantrell at The Cooper Union, and to Michael Rock and Sheila Levrant de Bretteville at Yale.

I wrote much of this book in the Frederick Lewis Allen Memorial Room at the Research Libraries of the New York Public Library. My thanks to Wayne Furman, its administrator, and to David Berreby, who kept me company there.

For my mother

Contents

Contents

Contents

Introduction

The color you see on my head is not the color that grows out of it. Peroxide is my life partner: I *choose* to be a blonde. Over the years, I've been an ash blonde, a sun blonde, and a platinum blonde. I've been a California blonde, a smart blonde, and an armpiece blonde. I may safely say, owing to my years of personal experience, that nobody knows blonde like me.

This love affair with blonde hair has had its rough patches. One of these occurred a few years ago when I was a graphic designer in New York. Tired of working, I decided to go to a very ritzy grad school to learn about signs and symbols and what they meant. At the time I was being a sunny blonde with warm honey highlights. I entered a graduate-school class of small, dark, honest brunettes.

For two years I learned about signs and symbols and about what advertising is doing to our culture and about how the media affects the way we think about ourselves. I read obscure dark-haired French philosophers and played chess long past midnight. I argued with old Marxist designers and lived next door to a jazz saxophonist. In short, I got an education. And yet I remained a blonde.

Real education is a radical process. It thumps you on the head until everything you know makes no sense anymore.

Then you run around picking up the pieces of your head and putting them back together. The pieces never go back together in the same way. When I put my own head back together after learning about signs-and-symbols and about how-the-media-affects-the-way-we-think-about-ourselves, the first thing I thought was that I didn't know why I liked being a blonde. And I wanted to find out.

When I turned the klieg lights of my education on the idea of blonde, I began to ask myself questions. Why did I desire blonde? Why do so many women want to be blonde? What did the symbol mean? I had to get to the roots of the matter.

Putting the prism of thinking in the path of blonde broke it into a thousand shimmering blondenesses—different kinds of blondes, different reasons for being blonde, blondes from the past, ancient protoblondes—the subject exploded. First I tried to figure out where the image of the blonde comes from, and then I began looking at different kinds of blondes—at who they are and at what they mean. For a blonde is a symbol just as assuredly as a unicorn is a symbol or a cigar is a symbol. But a blonde is never just a blonde.

The first thing I noticed, when I started looking at blonde-ness, was that the ebb and flow of my own personal blondeness follows a set pattern, which corresponds to the seasons of the year. Perhaps you, the blonde reader, have noticed the same repetitive yearning in yourself. Or you, the blonde-lover, have noticed this cycle in a blonde close to you. Let us review this annual cycle before all other symbolic delving, for it is the primary story of blonde.

It starts simply enough. Somewhere toward the end of winter, I catch a glimpse of myself and am suddenly overtaken by a feeling that a few natural-looking "sun-kissed" highlights are just what I need to feel better. At this very moment, being blonde and living in the real world start climbing their separate trajectories away from each other. For the idea of the weak New York winter sun kissing my hair is nothing short of ridiculous. (In winter, the sun never hits a strand: I scurry out to the laundromat with my head completely wrapped in wool scarves.) Here the fantasy begins.

I get a shiny, laminated, highlighting kit from the local drugstore, don its plastic cap, pull pieces of my hair out of the little, tiny holes with a crochet hook, apply a severe-looking blue paste, wait forty minutes (during which I wander around the house looking like a World War I aviator with hair transplants), and voilà—natural-looking sun-kissed highlights. I feel cheerier, though no one else notices.

A few months later, as spring pushes up the first tulip shoots along the paths of Central Park, highlights are suddenly not enough. I begin to crave a more meaningful blonde, and decide to go for the "full-head application," a commitment of time and resource similar to that of the average 401(k) plan. This time around, all the hairs on my head will have their moment with peroxide. I make an appointment at Irene's Hairstylist.

Irene's, conveniently located near my Upper West Side home, has many virtues. The average age of the clientele is eighty-one. Walker parking is provided in the front of the salon. This context makes me feel sprightly and youthful. The energetic, second-generation manager knows everyone and the thirty-year history of each woman's hair. There is no thumping music, black linoleum, or condescending twenty-something Eurotrash hairdresser who got a cosmetology license so that he could pay the rent while exploring his sexuality at clubs after hours. No. Irene's is a calm and peaceful place devoted to hair and its color.

The hairdressers at Irene's, after so many years of covering so much white, are particularly adept at shades of blonde. My colorist, Nick, somewhere in his fifties, has male-pattern baldness, wears a sensible blue smock, gives a manly shampoo, and goes home to Greece to visit his family twice a year. He has known me and my cycle of blonde for years, but always acts as though we are embarking on a new adventure when I appear in April.

We begin. After our yearly discussion of tints, he applies number 7A, Dark Ash Blonde, the tint I always decide on. I sit quietly among the Lucite hair dryers with a viscous violet goop on my head, and, after a wash and blow-dry, leave Irene's a confident, serious, dark ash blonde. April fades and May begins. I slowly realize that the operative word in dark ash blonde is "dark." Dark is not the blonde I care about. Denial of this situation lasts for some weeks, until friends convince me that I look pale.

In June, after a brief period of deep personal questioning on the topics of honesty and identity, I decide to go blonder. Turning back now would be too soon, for I have not achieved the true thrill of blonde.

I return to the walkers and to Nick. Nick suggests "blonde on blonde." I agree. We put frosted highlights on top of the 7A hair, a process that leaves me reading *McCall's* and *Ladies' Home Journal* for five hours with a plastic bag clothespinned to my head in the company of similarly accoutered octogenarians. I go home. My hair is blonde: a nice, comfortable, realistic, Connecticut blonde. June goes and July comes.

By August, I have lost all need for realism. Blonde lust is mounting in my heart. I want blonder blonde. Nick reminds me that I will have to submit to "double-processing," a step financially akin to the cost of a major kitchen renovation. At this point, I would immediately agree to any procedure guaranteed to make me the blonde I want to be. Caution is thrown to the winds. Wearing a face mask and gloves for protection, Nick removes all the natural pigment from my real hair, bleaching it dead white, then replaces it with a color called Lightest Winter Wheat #10.

It takes. At last, I achieve blonde. No brassy highlights, no realistic streaks, nothing to temper the gorgeous illusion of it all. I look like a light sheaf of wheat for two weeks in early September. And what a luxuriously blonde two weeks they are, for in every photograph I am blonde. At every dinner party I am blonde. In every plate-glass window I am blonde. I don't examine questions of personal identity. I am too busy responding to admiring glances from dark and interested-looking men at the fruit market.

But soon the inevitable starts to happen. My scalp, ravaged by ammonia and peroxide, begins peeling. Scar tissue becomes a real possibility. Suppressed thought intrudes. By October, turning to Irene's for help, I find that Nick is off surveying near his country home for the outbuildings that I have financed. Suddenly, the mental balance tips. I curse my blind and foolish pursuit of blonde. I total my monetary outlay. I begin to miss my real personality. I grab a box of hair color from the drugstore and color the exhausted hair on my head back to brown. It is November. I am myself again. I cook a turkey and wear long flannel dresses. When remembrance has worn, I will start the process all over again.

I am addicted to blonde. But I know that I am not alone in my addiction. Even the darkest of my friends has suffered through at least one ill-fated try at highlights, though by now most of them have adopted a stance of blonde refutal and castigation. Sour grapes, say I. Those two wheat-sheaf weeks are worth all the trouble, if properly scheduled, for during that time I am power and sex personified. I am fecund, I am ample, I am fearless. I believe my lines don't show as much. I catch the super looking at me admiringly while he's fixing the toilet float. The threat of future hospitalization with my scalp in a sling is nothing compared to the response I believe I see in others when I go really blonde.

I have succumbed to the power of blonde from the beginning. My poor hair is caught in the push and pull of a love affair with a goddess—a brilliant, bipolar goddess—for blonde is the manifestation of a great myth of our culture. My hair has been seduced by her and then given her up for good, time and time again. The experience of blondeness is the experience of trying to remember a wonderful dream, of trying to cast illusion in concrete, of grasping at gratification while dodging disappointment. No matter how much I enjoy the natural "me-ness" of the unadulterated me, I somehow find myself shouldering closer to the dream, closer to the image of blonde that we see in the movies, in advertisements, on TV. No matter where I am or what I am doing, deep down, I always want to be a blonde.

The Drugstore Goddess

It started naturally enough. I had the white hair as a child, and the streaming hippie-poetess blonde hair at twelve. But along about that time something started to happen, and it wasn't planned.

My hair got darker, finally ending up "dishwater" blonde, as my Southern grandmother used to call it. I am naturally dishwater blonde to this day, but even then, deep down in my psyche, I was blonde as sun.

The first thing you need to know about blondes is that you don't know any real ones. Not in your neighborhood, unless you happen to live upstairs from a Finnish tango parlor. Real, adult, fully functioning, totally blonde women are very rare, as rare as albinos. Remember this: Real platinum blondes have ruddy skin and give the distinct impression of having no eye-brows.

The day I finished the first draft of this book, I handed it to a messenger and got on a plane to California. After I landed, and was waiting for a bus, what showed up next to me at the bus stop but a real, honest-to-goodness platinum blonde, the second real platinum blonde I had sighted in all the time I had been thinking about blondes. I took it as a good omen. As the bus appeared, I said, "Excuse me, but I just wrote a book about blondes and, well, I just wanted to tell you that your hair is really beautiful. Natural, isn't it?" She turned her head and looked at me, expressionless. "Nice 'n Easy 100," she said, and boarded.

I only know one naturally platinum-blonde woman, and she lives in Kemijärvi with her large, naturally platinum-blond husband. They are a charming couple, in the reindeer meat business. These are not the blondes you know. The blondes you know are highly altered, and, whether they know it or not, they are all imitating the most exalted, terrifying, and annoying female icon of our century.

Even if the waif supermodel of current longing doesn't touch up the lights herself, she stands on the ample shoulders of Those Who Did. She wouldn't be where she is today if it weren't for Marilyn, Doris, and Brigitte. The blonde you think of when you think of blonde is a blonde soaked in hydrogen peroxide.

Do you think you are really a natural blonde? Take the test.

1. You believe deep down that after a week in the sun your natural hair would "bleach out" to a sun-tossed mane. Yes or No.

2. Tell us what actually happened that time in Martinique when you thought you'd just let the sun blonde you right out. Mention that after seven days in the broiling sun you could find only three blonde streaks and those may have been left over from a frosting kit. Mention your remaining dark undergrowth. Do not omit the extra hours spent with your head in saltwater. Do not omit the juice of those forty-three lemons.

○ ○ ○

If you want to ask a woman close to you if she is a totally natural blonde, you must make sure that you use those exact words, "a totally natural blonde," allowing no room for interpretation. Of course she might just flat out and out lie to you, because there's a kind of blonde that does that sort of thing. But if she is an honest woman, she will probably respond with the phrase "I was blonde when I was four."

"I was blonde when I was four," roughly translated for the layman, means, "Since I was once blonde, I have the right to strip the color from my hair, and to replace it with a color more akin to the longings of my true soul. I do this not to give a false impression of who I am, but rather to show the real me. I color my hair in order to bring it back to its *natural* state of blondeness." This is the rationale that works for me.

And so you ask the next question, "Why in the world would a woman go to such effort just to be blonde?" Simply put, she wants to live to tell the tale I tell, she wants to live the blonde life.

Generally, the difference between my day-to-day blonde life and the day-to-day brunette life is not extreme. It is manifested in a gentle rise of the tidewaters of public friendliness. People routinely smile at me on the street for no reason. Subway conductors hold the doors until I am on the train. Taxis stop for me when I'm not hailing them. The owner of the New Wave Diner, where I eat my daily Florentine omelet, kisses my hand every morning.

But it is the peak blonde moment that divides the mousy sheep from the lambent goats. It is true, I have caused minor traffic accidents. More than once, I have been randomly picked from crowds to say short lines in movies. And then there was that perfectly normal-looking guy in a Brooks Brothers suit who dropped to his knees in front of me one day on Wall Street and begged, "Oh, baby, just give me one chance."

These things don't happen because I am a quiet, polite person who can quote the first twenty-four lines of *The Canterbury Tales*. They do not happen because I pay my taxes and try to do right by my fellow man. They happen because I'm a blonde.

There's a difference between having blonde hair and being *a blonde*. A woman with light hair is not necessarily *a blonde*. Being African-American, Latino, or Asian doesn't keep you from being *a blonde*. Your gender, whatever you choose it to be, doesn't preclude you from being *a blonde*. Blonde is a hair color. But *a blonde* is a symbol.

Hair language is a valuable tool. Learning it will keep you

out of trouble, or get you into trouble if it's trouble you're looking for. When a woman decides to be a blonde, she is deciding
to stand for something, but what? Tina Turnerness or Marilyn
Monroeness? Pamela Anderson Leeness or Barbara Walters-
ness? Lisa Kudrowness or RuPaulness? If you look at a
woman's hair, it will tell you everything about what she
believes herself to be, deep inside.

If you can identify the hope that leaps up in a woman's heart
when a soignée European colorist pulls her head back, runs his
hands through her hair, slants his eyes, and says, "Darling, you
could be . . . a blonde!," then you have got the dossier on a
woman's deepest desire for herself.

o o o

This is not to say that the blonde life doesn't have its low
moments. I had one recently. My friend Laurel decided we
should take a film class. She thinks I should get out more.

There were thirty people in the class: beautiful nineteen-
year-old art girls and silent nineteen-year-old art boys; a Native
American guy who could repeat all the words to "Highway 61
Revisited"; Peter, the craggily handsome tofu magnate; and
Chantal, whom Laurel and I decided we liked because of her
intelligent eyes.

I originally had my eye on Peter, his being in the upper
range of my demographic, but backed off immediately when
Chantal-of-the-Intelligent-Eyes was spotted having pizza with
him during the break.

So I turned my full wattage on the professor. He was tall

and brilliant and downtown and lithe, and I spent the next few class sessions working my blonde hair to full advantage in his presence. I answered questions insightfully, and threw furtive, moist looks. Really made a darn effort. Nothing. Not a word, not a look, not a moment. I worried that he was the kind of professor who dreams of watching Pre-Raphaelite twenty-three-year-olds wander about in misty autumnal orchards. But I did not give up.

We watched a film by Tarkovsky—the film where everybody is whispering in Swedish about how boring it is to lie about in a very attractive seaside vacation house while the postman slowly rides around on his bicycle joking about Hegel, and young girls with towels on their heads get chased by geese.

After all this I went home, slept, and dreamed. When I awoke, I felt I had had a vision. I wrote our lithe professor a long E-mail about the movie. To my deep satisfaction, he E-mailed me back and asked me to review my ideas in the next class. He wanted the other students to reap the benefit of my deft insights.

At the next class meeting, I recapped my views, jumping nimbly from filmic metaphor to filmic metaphor as across stepping stones on a pond. "Tarkovsky believed," I said finally, "that salvation of the Self and of our world is only possible if the imbalance between our patriarchal societal constructs and our deep need for the greater spiritual consciousness of the mystical feminine is resolved."

I said this in a halting voice, with a certain amount of appropriate and totally feigned shyness. Silence fell. I felt that the other students were overcome by my observations. I also felt that I had given a real shake to the autumnal apple tree. But then Peter broke the silence. Turning to Chantal, he shook his head wearily. "That blonde is *nuts*," he said. I thought he said it quite loudly. But Laurel swears she barely heard a thing.

As I said, it was a low point. But I bring it up because it reminded me that there are two kinds of people in the world: the kind who look for symbols and images and metaphors, who find a reason for life in all the subtle ways that humankind makes meaning, and then the people who think that everything in life is like the train schedule for the New Haven line. Read across, read down, and there is your answer.

If you are the train schedule type, I am sorry. But I offer hope. If you look at a blonde and see only a blonde, stop yourself immediately, and remember where you put down this book. It will help you nudge open a few doors.

But if you look at a blonde and she is a blonde who talks— maybe a good game, a smart game, a game you don't understand completely; if you're tempted to call her crazy, and can't map her motivations; if her behavior is erratic, nonsensical, unscheduled—buddy, this is not the time to read across and down. Here's your chance to find out what blonde means, to dream one of the dreams our culture has for itself. Take a deep breath, toss out that train schedule, think metaphor, and come with me.

o o o

Today I went to the drugstore down the block in order to avoid working on my huge and complex never-to-be-understood-until-I-am-long-dead book, which is tentatively titled: "What All the Images in Advertising Mean Deep Down and How They Are Making You a Slave to Consumerism and Various Other Plots." It's my update of Casaubon's "Key to All Mythologies."

I wandered around hoping that someone would appear in the detergent section and offer to take me away to a small, breezy isle near Venezuela. Nobody showed. So I went over to the hair-care aisle.

There I gave myself up to comparing and contrasting the packaging of various hair-color brands, wondering whether the $9.98 box would give my hair more luster and sheen than the $7.96 box. I was drawn to a particular package. A long-haired blonde basked in Photoshopped sunlight as a little breeze played with the tendrils around her face. The type in the upper left-hand corner read "Lightest Summer Wheat Blonde."

I felt a familiar tug at my heart. I wanted to be that blonde, that blonde in that breeze, in that sunlight. I knew the box contained the same old two ounces of peroxide, but I didn't care. I wanted to own that lightness, that summer, that wheatness, that blonde.

o o o

In an office on the thirty-first floor of a gray building overlooking Fifth Avenue sits Max, a twenty-seven-year-old marketing manager who spends sixty hours a week thinking up hair-color names alongside his depressed and Zolofted brunette boss,

Janet, who worries about shelf presence and hasn't had a date since 1986.

A small army of hair-color namers is working in America today. And they're all trying to name their hair colors something that will make you tuck their box under your arm, lower your head, and charge to the checkout counter.

I wonder if Max and Janet have any idea that the blondes they invent are drenched in mythic symbolism. The words these two choose have been used to describe the power of the female from the beginnings of Western civilization. Does Janet blow through a copy of Turville-Petre's *Myth and Religion of the North* right before the marketing meeting, just to brush up on the blonde's role in Celtic heathendom? I would guess not. I would guess that the names they pick for blonde resurface in the culture the way saltwater lakes give up their dead. Sooner or later, certain words and mythic personalities bob to the top.

Next time you're at the drugstore take a real look at the names on those hair-color boxes. Together, they describe a fragmented whole: They describe what our culture considers the mystery of the mythically female. They paint a picture of the Heroine with a Thousand Haircolors.

The ancient goddess religions show their faces in the clichés on a drugstore shelf: They show their pretty faces, and they show their faces of greed, hunger, and desire. Ten thousand years of images stand right behind the idea of blondeness.

In the West, the power of woman must wear a mask in order to fit into the mainstream—in order to fit into the box provided. Whether that box is a television set or a movie screen or a magazine layout or a hair-color container, one of the most used masks in America is the mask of blonde. And one way to get hold of the image of the blonde is to sort her into categories, the way they sort seed pearls. To this end, I went back to the drugstore with a small pad and a pen.

As it turns out, the most popular blonde on the drugstore shelf is the Golden Sunlight Blonde. She commands a good half of all the shelf space in the blonde hair-color section. The runner-up is the Summer Wheat Blonde. She is followed by a gaggle of related blondes that make up a third category including Winter Wheat Blonde, Misty Starlight Blonde, Palest Moonglow Blonde, and (slouching from doorway to doorway), Warm Sherry Blonde and Champagne Blonde. Stepping smartly along behind all the rest, pushing a pram, is the sweet and doddering Pastel Blonde, and in that pram are the Innocents: Whisper-soft Blonde and Lightest Sun-kissed Baby Blonde.

Three kinds of blonde exist in the hair-color universe: Sun Goddesses, Moon Goddesses, and Innocents. There are a few half-breeds about—Innocents with Moon Goddess streaks, Sun Goddesses with Innocent highlights. But generally you'll be able to point them out on the street: She's a Sun, she's a Moon, she's an Innocent.

All blondes start out as Innocent Blondes. Some try to stay that way. But when they start coloring their hair, most women go one of two ways. Either they try to match their current hair color, or they try to show something about themselves. And that "something" can change. If, at the moment that you buy the box, there's something in you that wants to nurture life and culture, your hair will go Sun Blonde. But if at that particular moment there's something in you that wants to defenestrate the cat, you'll go Moon Blonde.

With the help of ammonia and peroxide, one month you can be a sun-wheat-and-growth blonde, drenched in honeyed tones. The next, you can be a sun-gold-and-purity blonde, diamondlike in your cool brilliance. After a particularly bad patch, you might spend some time as a champagne-colored moon-haze-and-liquor blonde, and then punch in at the office one day with hair the color of a towheaded toddler. In our time, women use their hair to telegraph their feelings about their innocence, their loss of innocence; about their sexuality, their eroticism; about getting older, about the prospect of death. The part of your personality that wants to say something very large speaks through the blonde you choose. The words of the goddess that want to come out of your mouth often get tangled in your hair.

o o o

When I was seven or so, my mother kept an old trunk as a permanent fixture on the screened back porch of our house in Virginia. It was our dress-up trunk, and held all her old cocktail dresses, pillbox hats, and high heels; some embroidered taffeta ball dresses from the relatives in San Francisco; and one or two moth-eaten mink stoles with glass eyes and snouts and tails. The neighbors got used to seeing two or three children walking down the sidewalk dressed like operagoing dowagers from Pacific Heights.

One day I decided that the dress-up trunk looked particularly inviting, with its soft old silks and deep velvets and bright satins. I climbed in to luxuriate. As the trunk lid closed, I heard a serious click, and, though it dawned upon me that I was locked in the dress-up box, I felt that someone would find me eventually, and promptly went to sleep. After a while, my grandmother noticed that I wasn't around, and began to search for me and to call my name. It was her calling that finally awakened me and caused me to sit up and bump my head and wail, attracting her attention. I remember the look on her face when she opened the trunk to find me howling in taffeta. I didn't know why she looked at me that way, I only knew she hugged me to her, and rocked me as I wailed.

We blondes are locked in the dress-up trunk. All those pretty colors, all those people to be. Like the waters of Lethe, they lull us, and we pass our lives away pretending to be people we are not. Fifty years ago, average women did not have the option of playing someone else, of coloring their hair. A hundred years ago, a woman was disparaged if she "painted," if she wore makeup. No makeup and no hair color and no one to be but yourself.

But now we want to be someone else, sometimes an alter ego, sometimes our "perfect" Self. We'll have the eye-lift and the chin implant and the breast enhancement. We color our hair and wear our makeup. But whom do we choose to look like? And what do our choices tell us about ourselves? These are the questions I asked myself in the drugstore, standing there with the boxes.

Innocent Blonde

I was blonde when I was four. We lived near Paris. My father was a diplomat, up to his ears in the Cold War. My mother was trying to figure out the French school system and how to call a plumber. I recall tangles. We drove a pumpkin-colored 1957 Plymouth station wagon with fins. In short, we were Americans.

I am one of the lucky few who had a childhood. Had it gone on for too long, I'm sure it would have palled. But childhood is brief, and therefore charming.

I remember few things from that time: My mother vainly trying to make a snowman from some unusual and un-Parisian snow. A dream of huge and beautiful butterflies flapping slowly around my nursery in technicolored brilliance. But mostly I remember hanging out in the house, having refused to go to the French nursery school after one disastrous morning of alienation and personal defeat.

We lived in Vaucresson. Our rented house had never seen a renovation. Built sometime in the 1800s, it smelled mustily of a bygone grandeur. In the kitchen, part of the floor was still scorched, and ironwork under the window still broken from the night that occupying Nazis lost control of a flaming kerosene stove and tossed it out into the garden. The rusted heap was still there in 1961.

That garden looked as big to me then as two acres look to me now, but it was just a decaying town yard, mapped by vines and pebbled paths around old espaliered apple trees that had been badly neglected. A German machine gunner's bunker still stood at the far end of the walk, built in the middle of someone's prewar border of banked perennials. In spring the pillbox floated in a sea of Queen Anne's lace.

Amid all this cultured decrepitude there was a gardener, my friend The Algerian. He had no other name. He arrived one day not long after we'd rented the house and, gesticulating with a pair of loppers, repeated the name of our landlady over and over until my mother hired him. The Algerians were still fighting the French; he looked like he needed the work.

The Algerian was about thirty-five, and had a laissez-faire attitude toward plants. He interfered only if something started to look ominous or foreboding. Upon his arrival each week, he walked silently around the perimeter of the garden, surveying the current situation. I always followed two steps behind him, explaining everything, while he kicked a bit at the lavender bushes, bent to throw a stone back onto the path, or leaned on his rake to watch the French clouds idle across the French sky.

The Algerian taught me how to eat flowers. We spent afternoons sitting on the bench, sharing roses, discussing the hostile personality of my pet rabbit or the difficulty of running on grass in new shoes. I told him everything and he told me some things, but he never said why the stove was in the side yard, or what happened in a revolution. And I did not know what evil was, and thought that the bunker was a little house at the end of the garden, a house with small windows.

o o o

The first face of blonde is the face of innocence. When we see the blonde tendrils on a baby's neck, we hope again. But innocence has a short shelf life in our culture, and soon the layers of experience start to lacquer even the littlest among us.

My seven-year-old niece turned to me recently and suddenly said, unprompted, "I am *so* over it." Perhaps she was just trying out the phrase. But she *is* over a lot: Barney has come and gone, so has Dad; a small truckload of little plastic Barbie things; *The Little Mermaid, The Lion King;* the baby-sitter who got killed in a car accident; Grandmommy; and those *Anastasia* toys from Burger King.

After early childhood, innocence mostly exists in memory, in pictures, and in fairy tales. But to soothe ourselves, we have invented a grown-up blonde woman-child: Our Innocent Blonde is a symbol of everlasting childhood.

This is her profile: She has the hair color of a six-year-old playing with a pail and shovel on the beach. She is not sexual or carnal: You'll never see her dig into a blood-red sirloin. She is often portrayed as virginal, though she may give birth to children. She does not do laundry. She may get married, but we never see her in the day-to-day of a relationship—in fairy tales, her story usually ends with her wedding. She lives happily ever after. She never dies.

Whether in Grimm's fairy tales or *Glamour* magazine, you know you are in the presence of an Innocent Blonde if she has a protector, magical or human; if she lives in an enchanted garden; if she remains young forever.

She looks carefree, yet someone is always watching out for her. A dragon, perhaps, or an agent, or a movie mogul. There's someone back there, and she knows it. Gray-eyed Athene has her best interests in mind. The knight-errant holds her handkerchief. Samuel Goldwyn draws up her contract.

Innocent Blondes live in enchanted gardens. Sleeping Beauty pricked her finger, and slept while an impenetrable wall of thorns slowly grew up around her. Those thorns entombed her, but they also protected her. She did not grow old, she did not die, she just waited for the prince's magical kiss to wake her from her trance.

The Innocent Blonde is a virgin, the girl not yet separated from the safety of her father's house. She is not yet fully individual, does not carry the burden of her own destiny. The magical kiss is a metaphor for her loss of virginity: It brings her back to humanity, out of the land of arrested development.

After that kiss, Sleeping Beauty is back on the mortal time clock. The wall of thorns disappears and she gets married. In-law problems surface. The clock starts to tick, and she embarks on the road to partial face-lifts along with the rest of us.

Fairies—the slight, winsome beings that they were in the stories of Victorian England—may not have weighed in heavily on the scale, but they pack a magical punch as Innocent Blondes. They lived within the confines of their fairy kingdom, they obeyed the rules of fairydom, and when humans stumbled upon them, the fairies always had the upper hand.

Fairies often appear to be delicate, with translucent wings and disheveled blonde hair. They are childlike, can act perversely, tend to stomp their feet. They dance in fairy rings in the silent woods, and bathe in moonlit waters. They inhabit a timeless world, and live forever.

Innocent Blondes are not threatening. And, in myths and stories, they often act as communicators between the world of the spirit and the world of everyday. This blonde is the one who shows the path out of the dark wood and knows the way to the mystic places. There's always something winsome about her—as if she has misplaced something precious, and goes through the world looking for it. An ephemeral being who lives half in and half out of our reality, she disappears without a trace, or appears uncalled. In *The Divine Comedy,* Dante's long-lost Beatrice acts as his guide to Paradise. She frequently disappears when he turns away, only to be glimpsed at some higher peak, to which he clambers after her. She leads him where he cannot go by himself.

o o o

Nancy Honeychuck dropped by my apartment the other day, unannounced. Now, I live in New York, and in New York, people don't drop by unannounced. It's not a cup-of-sugar type of place. Usually, if you want to see somebody, a ritual of date-setting and -breaking must be performed before the two of you can so align your date books as to make the fated lunch.

To tell the truth, it was about four in the afternoon and I was in the middle of one of those tortured binges during which one stands in front of the mirror trying to figure out how a neck-lift would really look, and wonders if one could be taken seriously ever again by the academic world if one just did a little something around the eyes.

I was looking at the stomach I had somehow achieved through the eating of cheeseburgers, pancakes, and sesame noodles, while pondering the devastating fact that many five-months'-pregnant women looked svelte compared to me. Generally, I was thinking the usual welter of thoughts of Self when my buzzer rang.

Through the miracle of video surveillance, I saw a tow-headed woman peering into the camera as if into a Christmas ball, and, thinking I could win a tussle if it came down to that, I let her in. But, of course, self-defense was unnecessary because it turned out to be Nancy Honeychuck, whom I had not heard from in seven years.

Nancy is the only true Innocent Blonde over the age of twelve that I have ever known. She is five-four and spare, with the wiry grace of a retired ballerina. I met her in Providence, where both of us had gotten tangled up with some jazz musicians. She was sleeping on a bass player's couch at the time. Hers is a psychic virginity.

Nancy Honeychuck tends to quote Horatian odes at significant moments, has a firm grip on thermodynamics, speaks fluent German, and seems to have no family ties or social encumbrances. I never have figured out where she was born, how she was reared, or how she ended up in Providence. She has a British accent, but that's about all I can tell you.

She sat in my living room and drank tea properly from a teacup while I lay across the settee and complained about work, men, my continuing eviction battle, and the nature of my recent dry cough—appropriate subjects for a meeting of New Yorkers, but they did not vibrate at Nancy Honeychuck's frequency.

"I have bought a little house," she said suddenly in a final-sounding tone.

"You have?" said I, blinking at the disruption of my droning monologue of vice and self-pity.

"Yes. I have bought a little house on an inlet in North Carolina, and I have bought a kayak."

"A kayak?" I said, trying to focus.

"A kayak. And sometimes, when the moon is out, I pack a little satchel and a fishing rod, and I kayak out into the darkness, and across to an island in the inlet. And I camp."

"You camp?" I said, scrambling to turn down the chatter in my mind. "You camp, when your house is right there?"

"Just up the inlet, out of sight. I beach the kayak, and lie out on the sand, and watch the stars, and listen to the night wind."

She clasped her hands behind her neck and looked up at my ceiling for a moment.

"And in the morning I paddle back to my house. A marvelous invention, the kayak. I recommend it."

Then she stood up to go, so I stood up. I walked her to the subway, and gave her a token, and the lighted train car pulled noiselessly from the station, and she was gone.

o o o

Enchanted gardens can take many forms: Look through the pages of *Town and Country,* that magazine of the socialite's created world. W. B. Yeats thought that custom and ceremony were the only ways to keep a woman innocent and beautiful. Keep her from the outside world, he said, and school her in refinement and culture. These intricate teachings will keep her sweet.

Such celebration of mental foot binding can really be annoying, but when I add Innocent Blonde highlights, am I not agreeing to just this idea? I'm proving that I still believe that I can push innocence past childhood, and retain it artificially.

In our day, as in all days, money builds the walls of the constructed garden of innocence. A woman brought up with lots of money has a chance at the advantage of a long girlhood. She doesn't start working at twelve, have children by fourteen, know all the ins and outs of life and death before she blows out the candles on her sixteenth birthday cake.

Innocent Blondes live in a world in which time stops and starts unnaturally; they never age or die. Take a look at the J. Crew catalog. Those models are telling you a story, a story you read as naturally as you read a highway sign. "Buy from this catalog," the story goes, "and you can be winsome, frail, and protected. You will trade places with me, the Innocent One, have dewy, fresh, and perfect skin like mine, and stop time for yourself."

That catalog dream, in which women are forever walking through fields of wildflowers holding heavy, half-filled baskets and wearing long dresses and big hats, is a story all women understand. It is a story we want, far from the day care center and the mall's parking lot. The pictures in those pages show us an enchanted garden, one that we will never enter, no matter how many big hats we buy. As the Russian poet Fyodor Tyutchev said, we, "like the beggar, barred from garden graces, carry the summer burning at our backs."

Innocent starlets remain ever young on film: Film is an enchanted garden of the past. We watch the ghosts of dead blondes parade a flickering innocence in front of us, over and over, until they are emblazoned in our minds, until they are part of our everyday lives, our reference points, our compass. In America, stardom ensures everlasting life.

The first time I saw Mitzi Gaynor singing that she was in love with a wonderful guy—I must have been twelve or so—I remember thinking, "What is that old woman doing prancing around in those white shorts?" Happening upon that *South Pacific* scene on a movie channel recently, my first thought was, "When did Mitzi get to be so damn young?"

I am getting older. She is staying the same. Unlike me, she has a strange relationship with time, as do all film stars. I have hung up my white shorts forever, but hers will prance on in perpetuity. When the reference points start to recede into the distance, when the compass slowly starts to spin round and round, losing north, women seek the blonde of innocence to distract themselves from their own mortality.

o o o

The Innocent Blonde is celebrated for her wholeness. She is not sexual; she is often presexual or has somehow skipped sexuality altogether. In myths and religions that take their cue from the stories of the Hebrew Bible, this absence of sexuality keeps the Innocent Blonde from the taint of Original Sin. She is a virgin—mentally, physically, emotionally.

I am always impressed anew at the endurance of the symbol of the Virgin Mary. Twisted to fit all kinds of patriarchal regulations, she signs through the fog of rules—a great female semaphore of nurturance, comfort, and strength. For, after all, she is a manifestation of the Great Mother.

The idea of virgin birth was used to separate her from other women, reminding them that they did not have her power because they did not have her purity. And so the Great Mother, when she rolled through Christendom, rolled through in the guise of innocence, so that she could be accepted into the patriarchal church. Bending the female mother goddess to virginity was no small trick for the church fathers. They did, however, leave one thing undisturbed: The Virgin's power is in her secret, unviolated spirit. Just as the mother goddesses before her held the entire world within them—life and death, evil and good—the Virgin holds within her the secret garden that nurtures the godhead.

The Virgin Mary is often painted as an Innocent Blonde,

her hair illuminated in gold, her look shy. Theologians referred to her as "The Enclosed Garden," "The Mystical Rose," "The Vessel of the Spirit," and Faust, in his prayer to the Virgin Mother, calls her "Godhead's Peer Eternal." So she contains all of the three basic tenets of our Innocent Blonde within her own Self: She is her own garden, her protector lives within her, and time has stopped for her—she is eternal.

o o o

Since she is protected, the Innocent Blonde does not *need,* and this is the most attractive thing about her.

Personally, I am always attracted to people who seem whole within themselves. I feel comfortable in the knowledge that they won't suddenly start spewing out their hatred of various family members over what was supposed to be a nice, civilized, Thai dinner with the in-laws. I feel calm in their presence. I like it when people stand on their own two feet, and don't threaten to come crashing down on me like a branch-snapping sequoia of emotional need. This blonde doesn't ever do that. She is truly self-contained.

In her protection and waifdom, the Innocent Blonde doesn't need to be completed sexually, she doesn't need an emotional bond with another person. Her body is not forever pulling her away from herself, toward another. And since she doesn't fall prey to lusts or whims, she has not had to abandon wholeness. She is comfortably stuck in that last narcissistic state of child-hood: happiness with herself. Hers is the emotional satisfaction of the prepubescent child.

Real people are not whole. The entire emotional castle usually needs pointing by the time we reach twenty-five. By forty, the physical walls are collapsing, and a Tartar horde of root canals and knee surgeries begins to pound at the portcullis with blunt instruments.

It is then that we begin to *need* like crazy. We need our husbands, lovers, sisters. We need the guy who smiles at us where we get the film developed. We need a sitter, the friends in the quilt group, a wry remark from the woman on the bus.

Women imitate the sign of the Innocent Blonde for many reasons, but the greatest of these is need. Some want to show you their spiritual condition of innocence, like the blonde waif in *Daytrippers,* or Lisa Kudrow's ethereal blonde persona in *Friends.* Some are using their hair to signal their self-conceived role as muse, fairy, or angel. Often musicians claim this higher authority. I have to say, from where I sit, they are the greatest abusers of the Innocent-vision-for-marketing-purposes. Look at Jewel, who followed up her longing-waif music videos with a nice, longing picture of her longing self on the jacket of a thick book of longing poetry. And Courtney Love made an about-face recently, going from tough Seattle rock girl to wan muse via a trainer, a diet, and a good photographer. Even Madonna dashed through a spiritual Botticellian Venus-rising-from-the-sea moment with the release of a recent CD, but, in characteristic Madonna style, dyed her hair dark red and forgot the whole thing a year later. These musicians want you to believe that they have a connection with something spiritual, want to cash in on the need they feel reverberating in the dead air around them.

Sometimes women feel they have no spiritual or physical protector, are vulnerable, and want to create the condition that will lead to protection, to being whole and invulnerable, and so they imitate innocence. (Daryl Hannah plays this kind of blonde in *Splash*.) And sometimes a woman has just had enough of being banged around, and seeks solace in the blondeness of enchantment and otherworldliness. Deep down, this blonde is hoping that if she imitates the Innocent very, very well, time will stop, and she will never age and never die.

o o o

Men—men who are old and know they should know better—have always been attracted to Innocent Blondes. The waif-child does not put the burden of reality on a man; she asks for nothing. She doesn't bring up the necessity of home rodent abatement on car trips. She's not the reality of a wife, she's not the fantasy of a mistress—she is an illusion of never-ending youth. To her, this slightly aging guy fills the mythic role of protector. To him, she is one last chance. Have that girl, have that youth: Have freedom and eternal life.

Strangely, she symbolizes the same thing for women, although you'd think she'd just drive them ape, what with their husbands pining for her every chance they get. But she's not conniving or a femme fatale, and women like her, even protect her. She's the Ivan Durak of blondes: often odd, following a trail unmarked for others, walking through the world alone. In *Breakfast at Tiffany's*, Audrey Hepburn's dark hair is lightened with wise-child streaks, and her behavior is that of

Kipling's cat: She walks by herself, and comes to maturity only when she allows herself to need another person.

The Innocent Blonde inside every woman wants to kick over the traces every now and again. There are moments when we all get the urge to abandon the four-by-four by the side of the road, dump the kids off at the sitter's for fifteen years, pay off the mortgage with a flick of the pen, and make tracks for Aruba. But we can't, so we buy a box of hair color called Lightest Baby Blonde, and disappear into the bathroom for twenty minutes.

When the pressure is on, baby-blonde hair can suddenly look very good to us, and before we know it we're pulling out wispy tendrils and wearing watercolored chiffon dresses with skinny straps—straps that an errant flex of kid-lifting shoulders could burst in an unguarded moment. Of course, we don't realize that we're trying to regain innocence, trying to regain a phantom protection, trying to muscle our way back into the enchanted garden.

○ ○ ○

The Innocent Blonde is the bright child who gives the artist a reason. She links things: art and inspiration; truth and representation. The blonde in *As Good As It Gets* provokes art from a damaged painter and sanity from a crazed novelist. In Dante's *Divine Comedy,* it is Beatrice, the blonde embodiment of perfect love, who takes the poet up through heaven, and shows him what lies beyond.

Here we must talk about angels, because angels are wise

children with wings, and they are often painted as Innocent Blondes. Angels are beautiful, sexless, untroubled, pure. They are complete within themselves and at one with the rhythms of the celestial garden as they follow along comfortably behind the celestial Gardener. They are not embroiled in political infighting, watercooler chatter, or careerism. (Lucifer, king of watercooler agitation, is the exception who makes the rule here.) When angels do come down to earth, they have to look out for themselves, for they are in hostile territory and are a long way from home.

I thought about this a lot during the O. J. Simpson trial. Nicole's character was as manipulated by the prosecution as it was by the defense. The defense went to great lengths to describe her as a drug-addicted sex maniac who was a menace to her children and deserved her death because of her wayward life. The prosecution managed to ward off some of these attacks, but in the media, the view of Nicole as an irresponsible gold-digging blonde gained ground.

Soon after the character attacks began, members of Nicole's family appeared in the courtroom wearing small golden angel pins. Soon, anyone who was pro-Nicole wore one, including the DA. What a nice, neat, compact little symbol. What a smart move.

The person who invented the angel pin understood, consciously or subconsciously, the truth that the American public could never consider a sexually active separated woman as a victim. By downplaying her sexuality and likening her to an angel, the family altered Nicole's characterization in the media. Suddenly she began to take on the attributes of an Innocent Blonde.

She was a waif who had been turned out of her enchanted garden of Brentwood, whose protector may have turned on her in a myth-shattering way. In the end, Nicole was posthumously reinvented as an Innocent, one whose time ran out.

o o o

Nicole assumed the mythic role of Innocent after her death, as part of a court battle. But Princess Diana lived as an Innocent Blonde. It was her myth, shaped to her as to no one else. Her death was unexpected, foolishly accidental, and caused a public grief never before seen in the history of television. TV pundits were at a loss to explain this outpouring, retreating to the idea that Diana had been both a princess and a nice person, an unusual combination that had made her a special favorite of average women.

Yes, she seems to have been a good person, and it is true, women do like the implied fairy story of life as a princess. But Diana's death was an unnatural ending to the myth of the Innocent Blonde, and that unnatural ending is the key to the ravaged quality of the public's grief. She embodied the myth, but she broke the covenant. Instead of altering time, pushing back the clock or making it stop altogether, she broke with the story—she was killed in an accident. The whole thing was just inconceivable.

Diana kept keenly to her mythological type until that moment in the Mercedes under the overpass. We knew Diana for more than twenty years, and all of her life she was an Innocent Blonde: the fresh face in the ossified royal family. Virginal before marriage, she expressed her love of children in her work as a nursery-school teacher, and later as a nanny. After her wedding to Charles, which was hailed as the fairy-tale wedding of the century, she went off to a Scottish castle to begin her life in the enchanted garden of social responsibility and public facade.

Although celebrated, Diana was a private person, and her privacy was a part of her charm. Having been elevated socially to a public life, she did not have to seek the press, the press sought her. Her quest for privacy led to her death. Although the most photographed celebrity of her era, she was not known.

She was an Innocent: Though she wore black velvet dresses and diamond tiaras, she always gave the impression of a little girl dressing up in someone else's clothes. She did not ooze sexuality. Her attractiveness was in her freshness until her dying day. After her death, the pictures most prominently displayed had been taken when she was in her early twenties, not in her later, maternal years. Her eating disorders fit the myth, too, for Innocents are not carnal—she had a tendency toward wasting away rather than toward robust partying or debauchery.

She lived in the enchanted garden of her social station, but the usual protectors failed her. Her father died. Her husband was rippingly unfaithful. Diana's protector, her dragon at the gate, was a public that responded viscerally to the myth that she made real. The public was her magical guardian, coming to her aid at her divorce, appreciating her charities and volunteer work, understanding the frailties it saw and wanted to protect. That public grieved deeply when it lost its charge, for it had participated in her story. In faerie, the dragon that fails its mistress sheds its scales and creeps back quietly into its cave to die. But Diana's public had nowhere to go but to the gates of her family's estate.

Diana was a mirror for the dreams of international womankind. She was an emotional yardstick: She got married when we married, she had problems when we had problems. She survived as we had survived: She found new love, as we hoped to find it. The women of the world cried for Diana, but deeply they cried for themselves. They cried for the breaking down of the garden wall, for the truth that no human protector can prevent the finality of death.

Innocent Blondes have a strange relationship with time, and Diana is no exception. She will always be beautiful, young, and hopeful in the thousands of photos that chronicle her life. Her fair fame will not fade. The media that hounded her for the public that protected her will also give her a kind of immortality.

o o o

Like a child, the Innocent Blonde brings out the protective feelings in those around her. We want her to be happy in her garden, untinged by the strife of everyday life. This blonde gives us hope for the future, and we husband her just as we nurture a belief in Santa Claus: We want her world to touch our world and make it better. Jaded, cynical as we are, Innocent Blondes still inspire us to something greater than ourselves. They still point us in mystical directions.

Oh, That Strawberry Roan

By the time I knew her, my mother was not blonde. She wore her dark hair short and natural, like a Hemingway heroine. She had soft, hazel eyes and the high cheekbones of a Cherokee. There's a rumor that one or two sneaked into her Southern ancestry.

But blonde came striking through from the Russian side of the family, the side on which everyone was tall, and well-proportioned, and (in the old photos of hunting parties and picnics in the woods) always seemed on the verge of painting something snowy with birches or writing something Symbolist about the eternal battle of light and dark.

During the Russian revolution, these people got to be called White Russians, White as opposed to Red. The Whites who survived got out of Russia with nothing but their titles, and took whatever jobs they could get. The men drove taxis, washed dishes in bistros, or stood out in front of cabarets in outlandish doorman costumes.

There were still a few of these Russians around when we lived in Paris. I remember that one of the telephone operators at *The New York Times* was a princess by birth, and this caused my father, whose forebears had lost their principality in 1350, to get his military bearing on and start bowing toward the telephone every time he had to call the paper.

I have a Russian friend who says that he divides his acquaintances into two groups: those who have been shot at, and those who have not been shot at. "When a man knows he is to be hanged in a fortnight," said Samuel Johnson, "it concentrates his mind wonderfully."

These displaced Paris Russians had been shot at, and if they knew how to do one thing well, it was to celebrate the moment. My father had a number of far-off relatives in the emigré community. Consequently, my parents gave magnificent parties.

My mother, the South Carolinian, felt that a good party depended on plentiful food, soft lighting, and a carefully composed guest list. My father thought that a good party depended on at least one spontaneous performance by a brilliant violinist who just happened to be passing through town, and on a few Russian charades in which diplomats and ballerinas declaimed, sang, and acted out violent dramas, the men with their ties tied around their waists and steak knives in their teeth, the women with hats made of sofa pillows perched on their heads.

We did not consider it a good party unless someone fell in love. With two older sisters, this really was not such a tough thing to pull off. I remember Lita, a passionate nine years old, lying on a sofa in a swoon of love and concern when her English teacher, a distinguished elderly man of about twenty-five, inadvertently sat on a sewing needle during one of these parties. It was removed by my gracious mother's own hand in a secluded back bedroom.

The parties always started out stiffly. The French stood as silent as ice sculpture, the Americans clutched bourbon and waited. The Russians shuffled in, looking slightly paranoid and wishing they were wearing better clothes. But after a while, they all relaxed, and somewhere in the glow of candles and the second cocktail and the air of a late spring evening, all would meld into celebration.

Buttons unbuttoned, stories were told over the ice bucket, someone translated from Russian to English. Someone translated from English to French. The warm voices turned into a hazy buzz. And, under the table that held the chafing dishes, I sat in four-year-old bliss, a toothpicked cocktail meatball in each hand.

Much later in the evening the remaining guests settled onto sofas in a daze. After arguing about de Gaulle in three languages and striking a few intellectual sparks with those who knew their Sartre, they were comfortable and exhausted. The fire fell in embers, cognac went around. My father took up his guitar and we sang.

My father is Russian when he has to be, but in his deep heart he is a cowboy. Brought up in the States, he speaks with no trace of a Russian accent. His English is Western, and his heroes are too. Sooner or later, after the Russian songs, and after at least one pass at "Adiós, Muchachos" with an Argentine secretary, my father bent to a general urging and sang "The Strawberry Roan."

He first heard the song when he was eight years old, listening to a cowboy singer named Glenn Hood, sitting by a campfire in Yosemite. But over the years, he made the song his own. There in Paris, forty-four years old, with responsibilities shouldered and politics heavy on his mind, he took up that guitar, sang that song, and America came back to us.

o o o

The ballad tells the story of an out-of-work cowboy who bets that he can break the Strawberry Roan, the "sumfishin'ist critter" that ever was born. He lives to regret that bet. At four, I particularly liked the way my father worked his Russian name into the song. His cowboy was named Boris.

We all sang the chorus—the French bureaucrats, the Russian countesses, the American wives: Together we bemoaned the fate of the guy who gets on the Strawberry Roan.

Someone must have explained to me that a strawberry roan is a very light red horse, in effect, a strawberry blonde horse. My mother and father had dark hair. Lita was overwhelmed by auburn curls, and Nadia's light brown hair was short. My grandmother wore a grandmotherly white bun. The first blonde I ever knew, the first blonde I ever thought about, was the Strawberry Roan. That horse stole my heart. It was my first symbol, though I did not know what a symbol was.

But what did I know of anything in 1961? I barely knew the dandelions in the cobblestoned street, or the sluggish hop of my aforementioned rabbit, Mademoiselle Boussac. I didn't know that "Mademoiselle Boussac" was an odd name for a rabbit—I had no context within which to know. In the first light of morning, I heard the coal buckets scrape and could not identify the sound. I had never seen a coal bucket. I knew little of anything and nothing of blonde.

Blonde innocence and blonde experience have always danced together. The Innocent Blonde, the girl who is not awakened to sexuality, acts as a spiritual guide for the men who love her. But this strawberry roan blonde, this is another blonde entirely. A horse of a different color. This blonde represents the part of the mythic feminine that cannot be possessed, that will not be broken. And, to make matters even more interesting, this is an old blonde, a crone of a blonde, a crone wrapped in the skin of her animal nature.

The actual sex of the Strawberry Roan was vague. The idea of something male having to do with strawberries didn't quite feel right. Sometimes the song called it "she" and sometimes "he." Going with the line "thin in the middle and wide at the hips," I envisioned the horse as a "she."

But sexuality was a moot point for me. The thought of penis envy had never crossed my mind. (The thought of penises had never crossed my mind—this was a family of girls.) Thank goodness I was a voracious reader in later years or I might still need clarification on this point.

These days, horses are interpreted as phallic symbols: Since

Freud, they've dominated anxiety dreams and car ads, symbolizing unbridled power, potency, muscularity, strength, and freedom. The horse is akin to the motorcycle, power between the legs, and so forth. But unlike the motorcycle, the horse can also mean something mythically female.

Beryl Rowland, who writes about the mythic symbolism of animals, tells us that in the Middle Ages, the body of a horse was symbolic of sex and, for that reason, equated with woman. She says that courting a woman was often compared to buying a horse, and that many ancient proverbs remind a man to keep a tight rein on both his wife and his horse, or warn that well-traveled women, like well-traveled horses, are never trustworthy.

Robert Graves asserts that the ancient mother goddess of the Britons was a white horse goddess—Epona, the mare-headed Demeter. This goddess's cult, widely diffused in northwestern Europe during the Iron Age, went even farther during the time of the Roman Empire. Juvenal referred to her altars, and Giraldus Cambrensis, a clergyman who died in 1213, tells us that relics of the cult survived in Ireland until the twelfth century.

Rowland feels that this mother goddess Epona represented strength, power, and sexual potency, but was also the incarnation of the divine cycle of growth, death, and regeneration.

The Strawberry Roan was old. She was a hag of a horse. If she was a symbol of the mythically female, she was a symbol on her spavined last legs. Like the Russians at my parents' parties, she was looking down the barrel of destiny. She had been singled out to be broken, and not only did she resist, she triumphed. "The Strawberry Roan" was my first lesson in valor.

We Americans mythologize the unbroken while methodically trying to break down everything in sight. We love the free range, then map it with fencing; we love the wild rivers, then dam them for electricity. We love the unbroken bronco, but continue to try to break it. We love the fecundity, the power, of woman, and then we shut her in suburbia with a bonus room and an ice-making Frigidaire.

When my father sang about the Strawberry Roan, I sat there in a large-eyed trance. And of course I put him in the story. What did I know of Freud or Bettelheim or fairy tale or myth? What did I know of the horse as sexual symbol? Was I aware of the dire psychological drama inherent in picturing one's father trying to break a blonde horse? I was four. Later I would macramé the psychological threads. But for now, my father got the part of the cowboy.

Myths are cultural stories: They teach us who we are, how to react to things, how to be. "The Strawberry Roan" was the first mythic story I ever heard. It told me something I needed to know about the female in our culture, it told me something about the male.

This myth, like most Western myths, has a hero. To paraphrase Joseph Campbell's definition, it has a character who goes somewhere, learns something, and returns with knowledge that can help his fellow man. A "hero" story is about the quest and about the return. A "heroine" story, however, is about something else.

Reading "The Strawberry Roan" as a hero story, we watch

the self-assured cowboy betting that he can break an old, ornery horse. At the end of the song, the horse takes one last leap and, as the broncobuster puts it, leaves him "sitting on nothing, way up in the sky." He falls, loses the bet, and tells us about it. That's the plot. It's not convoluted, but it does the cultural job. The lesson: "Don't be an idiot. There are beings in nature that are wilier and tougher than you are."

o o o

In the hero story reading, the cowboy loses the battle with the Strawberry Roan, but acknowledges nature's victory over him and gives honor to his honorable opponent. By honoring the horse (by cussing it out, in this case), he shows that he understands his own rightful place in the hierarchy of the natural world. He has learned his limits; he has, at least for the moment, replaced his pride with humility and has found a truer identity. When the man is the hero, our Strawberry Roan is an agent of the man's self-reappraisal and growth. And that's what this little story is supposed to be about.

But when I was four I didn't see it that way. I thought that the song was centered on the Strawberry Roan. The horse was the heroine, the man was the foil.

I thought that the man existed only in order to bring out the inherent valor of the horse. "Men," as my friend Sara-Lynne once said, "may just exist in order to antagonize the poetry out of women." If the cowboy did not exist, the horse would have had to invent him, because its tenacity, daring, and unbrokenness can be expressed only when the cowboy gets on its back.

A heroine story is about being able to endure. In primitive cultures, boys are initiated into manhood by setting off alone into the darkness, hunting an animal, killing it, and returning triumphant. But girls pass to womanhood by being shut up in an enclosed space and showing their bravery by enduring the pain of initiation rituals.

The male side of the psyche accomplishes, the female side endures. Getting these two sides of the mind to work together can look a lot like a three-legged race. The team that establishes unity wins.

They need each other, the cowboy and the Strawberry Roan. Without her, the cowboy's pride keeps him off balance, untempered, untaught. Without him, the blonde horse can't show her valor. She is old, wily, and difficult, but so admirable—admirable in a cussed sort of way.

The Semi-Dior Pivot

I got my first blonde goddess training the year I turned thirteen, the year I grew six inches and ate an entire standing rib roast by accident, as a snack, while reading *Jane Eyre*.

My parents retired from the diplomatic life, and we moved to the Bay Area, where I'm sure my father envisioned embarking on a calm and relaxing second career—daubing at the watercolor in the morning, fine-tuning the novel in the afternoon, wielding the ice tongs on the patio by five P.M.

But it was 1969, and we moved west just in time to catch Angela Davis, the Symbionese Liberation Army, and the drug-addicted remains of flower power. My mother suddenly began making velvet patchwork pillows, and one of my father's friends appeared on the doorstep one day wearing purple bell-bottoms and proclaiming, "Stop the world, I want to get off!" Still, aside from these small rumbles, few cultural tremors rattled our suburban house.

I was wearing Villager shirtwaists and penny loafers when we moved west, but the friends I made were northern California suburban girls, and they immediately set me straight. Within days I was wearing a light-blue polyester crepe blouse with huge leg-o'-mutton sleeves, hip-hugger brown corduroy jeans, and a belt with an enormous belt buckle that said "Marlboro." I was parting my long blonde hair in the exact middle and wearing love beads.

We were all tall, my girlfriends and I. Leslie leveled off at five-ten, Nancy at six feet. I was six-two before anyone noticed that I was getting kind of tall.

When I silently grew past all the others in my ballet class, the teacher turned to my mother and shook her head with unmistakable finality. This was bad. But the top shelves in the kitchen, where my mother hid Mars bars, were suddenly conveniently at eye level. This was good. I was taller than she was, and taller than my sisters. Yet she remained calm, for she was not a woman prone to alarm.

Still, there was tall and there was too tall. During an afternoon tea with the Russian relatives in our velvet-patchwork-appointed living room, my czarist Russian grandmother turned to my mother with an air of icy authority and intoned, "Natalia must not grow another inch!"

It was then that my mother started me thinking about creating a mythic persona for personal use. As she explained it, there were only two ways I could go. Either I could wear big, flat shoes and slump about for the rest of my life with my hair in a bun, or I could train to be a woman who looked as if she had altered her DNA to her own purposes. I could train to be a goddess. The choice was not as simple as you may think.

There's a lot to be said for slumping about and being invisible. Visibility breeds notice. Notice breeds a call to leadership. Leadership requires decision making. Decision making can cause you to decide wrong. And failure stands out when you're tall. Tall blondes are easy targets for tomatoes.

Then there are all those difficult visibly tall moments: looking down on your boss when he's ranting at you, for instance, or being stoic when your current beau looks up and tells you he'd just rather go out with someone a little more, well, average size.

My mother was a beautiful woman. She entered rooms as if alighting from a cloud. "All eyes will turn to you," she used to say, "so be SPEC-TAC-ULAR!" At thirteen, I was about as spectacular as a gerbil. She sensed plummeting self-esteem. She saw big, flat shoes in my future. So she took an unthinkable step. She let me go to modeling school.

My mother was not a narcissist, and she did not value narcissism in others. She thought a woman should know her worth, but she detested vanity and always reminded us of how she'd watch the French diplomats' wives admiring themselves in the embassy dining room's mirrored walls.

Perhaps she thought that walking on a catwalk would banish the gerbil in me. So, to the dismay of the Russians, who believed that full-scale prostitution lay immediately around the corner, and despite a tragic lack of cheekbones, I went to modeling school.

My mother wanted me to look like a goddess, but to behave with a propriety not known in North America since the ante-bellum period. Her view of goddesshood left out all the good parts, all the parts that "A Child's First Book of Greek Myths" leaves out. Not for her the bathing in ferny bowers and then setting upon intruders with baying hounds. Not for her the vulgar Leda and the swan incident, or Priapus, or Zeus as a bull. It was just *not done*.

She just wanted me to grow into my feet. But I dreamed of stardom. As a model, I would be forever captured in my evanescent youth, and my nubile form would give value to large man-made products. If my measurements were right, if my features were regular, if I were physically perfect, I would get the great cultural nod of approval and would bathe in self-esteem.

If I could model, if I could attain modelhood, I would suddenly hop over the line between the human and the divine. For divinity, in our culture, is the attainment of the level of physical female perfection perceptible to an average man.

Unbeknownst to me, my mother and the woman who ran the modeling school locked steely gazes as the check was written out. They understood each other. There were to be no heroic measures in getting me in front of a camera. All this modeling hooey, my mother said in her gaze, was just so that I would stand up straight—nothing more, nothing less. Modeling, after all, is selling the use of your body for money. My mother knew it. The gal who ran the school knew it. At that time, it was the conventional wisdom in certain circles that selling the use of one's body for money was, shall we say, a last resort.

Now, of course, women think of their bodies as commodities. We think of ourselves as having a value somewhere between toilet paper and pig iron, depending on the current state of our self-esteem. And I don't know any woman, including me, who wouldn't do anything in front of a camera, given the right photographer. But those were simpler days.

The modeling school mistress, Ms. Luker, was an old model herself, about my mother's age. She had seen too much sun in her perfect youth, and her skin was lined and colorless. She had a size-eight figure, wore yellow pants and white tops, had a double-processed blonde pageboy the color of ginger ale, and smoked cigarettes to keep from eating. She could summon an outgoing, natural-looking smile on command. She was nice to me; she knew I was hopeless.

Models are found, not taught, but we, the raw recruits, did not know this. We thought we had a chance. Instead of telling us that we did not, the modeling school kept our hopes alive. A cruel ploy, but lucrative. We thought our success or failure depended on our willingness to adapt to the stringent Unspoken Precepts of the School. Precept number one was: "No matter what you weigh, you are too fat."

We were weighed. Scowls all around. All ten of us immediately went on the Atkins diet. At thirteen, I weighed 138 pounds, and was, as I mentioned, 6 feet 2 inches tall. Take a look at your 6-foot-2, 195-pound husband and tell me how fat I was. But I dutifully ate celery wrapped in ham slices to lose the ten required pounds. It was like eating bony fingers.

At this juncture I met Fat Ankles, a pert, blonde 32-22-32. She was petite. A fellow modeling student, I thought of her as much older than I was. She was fully formed, like Venus rising from the sea, born of the spume of waves. To me, sex was something in an Ian Fleming novel. To her seventeen-year-old self, it was a burnished tool. She had been voted Miss ROTC that year. She smiled a warm, totally false smile, sported a tiny waist, and had only that one obvious fault—legs by Baldwin.

Tall and short women have an aversion to each other, not unlike cats and dogs. Short women think tall women are tall on purpose, in a scheme to get noticed. Tall women are afraid they will hurt short women. I always marvel at the way their tiny hands work.

Fat Ankles was short, but she was as pretty as hell, and determined to be a model. She lived by the modeling school's Second Unspoken Precept: "Inner beauty is hogwash." In all my long years on the planet, I have yet to encounter another woman so completely without scruple, principle, or unselfish motive.

This was the woman who put rubber cement in other people's mascara so that hers would be the only long lashes and open eyes in the group shot. This was the woman who was caught sabotaging the heel of another girl's shoe in order to lame her on the runway. This was the woman who said to me, "Oh, let me stand by you, it makes me look so feminine!" She was a Moon Blonde, a particular kind of blonde, one we will profile later.

After we started our diets, Ms. Luker spent long, patient hours teaching us to walk (books on the head), to emerge from cars gracefully (large car prop in room), and to walk down stairs by lowering ourselves from step to step, using the weight-bearing quads to full advantage. Finally, she taught us the "Semi-Dior Pivot," a 360-degree modeling turn not in use today.

In those days the Semi-Dior was state-of-the-art modeling, a more "natural" adaptation of the famous fifties Dior Slouch, in which the model's hips preceded her shoulders by about ten paces. Our hips preceded our shoulders by only two or three paces, a modified, or "Semi-Dior," walk. These days I see a lot of the Androgynous-Storm-Trooper walk and the Foot-Crossing-Mambo walk, but in those days, we kept to the old Semi-Dior.

The Semi-Dior Pivot involves slouching halfway down a runway, turning all the way around in one quick motion (while making eye contact with all the photographers lined up on either side of the catwalk and letting the arms slap around freely), and then continuing to slouch down the runway as if nothing has happened. It can look like a little known form of Tourette's syndrome if done poorly.

I wore down the shag rug in our living room learning to do the Semi-Dior Pivot. To this day this turn comes in handy if I suddenly have to remove a roast from the oven in a small kitchen.

We pivoted, dieted, had our measurements taken every week, learned how to apply Pan-Cake makeup, individual false eyelashes, and "contour" (brown foundation that makes hollows where hollows should be). We learned how to pull up the fat on the sides of our thighs, pull up and push in our breasts, and hide our nipples with strategically applied strips of gaffer's tape, a sort of heavy-duty duct tape common on photo shoots. Finally we stood ready to be photographed for the first time. Many of the modeling school aspirants hired expensive photographers to take glossy, enhanced, color pictures of them lying about on cars. But I had no money, so my sister volunteered.

Strangely, Lita, then in high school, was a talented photographer. Too talented. She saw through the layers of advertising gloss in which I so desperately wanted to be embedded. She was a real portraitist, and this worried me.

But we gave it a try. First: a suitable background. We needed a feeling of quiet wealth and luxury. Our house did not cut the mustard. We thought of Mrs. Kittle.

Mrs. Kittle lived in a beautiful, huge, old Colonial Revival shingled house on the top of a hill. It was the kind of house that has a small marker stating its name at the beginning of its private drive. I always felt at home at Mrs. Kittle's. This worried my parents.

She was in her seventies at the time, living alone in her big house tended by a housekeeper. Her sons were long gone, off to where sons go. Age was affecting her mind in the strangest way: She was losing the ability to find words. She could understand anything you said to her, but she could not talk back.

But Lita and I liked Mrs. Kittle, and we knew she liked us, so we drove up the hill to take the modeling pictures at her house. Lita promised me she would try to make them as unrealistic and as glossy as possible.

And so somewhere, to this day, there is a picture of me at thirteen, wrapped in sable and backed up against Mrs. Kittle's slightly open front door in the come-hitherest of all come-hither poses. I remember Lita crouching against a prickly holly tree, trying to get in the right place to take the picture. I remember enjoying being the star of the moment, with fake eyelashes and Pan-Cake makeup. But mostly I remember that right behind me, against the other side of that front door, Mrs. Kittle stood, intent, stooped, and silent, using her body as a doorstop so that we could get the perfect picture.

Lita's photographs inspired a young male teacher's aide in my junior high classroom to expostulate, "I know *you*?" So I figured they were pretty good.

By the last week of modeling school, we had all learned the third precept: "Your future is in the hands of James Bouffet." Soon we would meet him, the head of the modeling agency.

As I saw it, this tiny birdlike man was the person who stood between my nowhere teenage life and the life of sun-shot stardom to which I aspired. He was the one who could make stacks of black-and-white head shots (featuring me) a reality. He was the one on whom I had pinned my dreams of lounging about Roman discos wearing Qiana evening dresses. It was James Bouffet whose very nod could whisk me off to New York and into the candids of parties with Halston that always ran in the back of *Vogue*.

The day of our meeting arrived. The ten of us stood in the seventies modeling school variant of military attention: the pose still used today at the end of Miss USA competitions. The stress was fierce. Perspiration threatened my Pan-Cake job. The tape holding up my thighs began to itch. I felt an individual eyelash blow off and stick somewhere on my cheek. But I had my portfolio of Mrs. Kittle's shots at the ready.

When James Bouffet saw my photos, he let out a plaintive cry and slumped, beaten in his quest for perfection. "What do these girls *think*?" he asked no one in particular. "Look at that! Is that supposed to be *hair*? Highlights! She needs highlights! Get those pounds off. Who's next?" His assistant duly wrote notes and handed them to me: "Lose weight to 119. Hair: no style, no color—needs blonde."

No style. No color. Needs blonde. I had failed. I would not be inducted into the ranks of the blessed. For days I lay on the shag rug in the living room and mourned. No New York. No Avedon telling me how much he loved my hands. No Paris, no Rome, no Milan. And all because I was fat and not blonde.

My mother looked silently at the Mrs. Kittle pictures, then silently at me. Her eyes told me that she wanted to kill James Bouffet. They told me she was furious at Ms. Luker for welching on their bargain and getting my hopes up. They also suggested that I get off the rug and think about someone else for a change. Her eyes showed her revulsion at the situation and her pity and her anger. But she said nothing.

o o o

James Bouffet and the Semi-Dior Pivot and the Mrs. Kittle pictures remind me of what happened when Zeus and Hades conspired to kidnap Demeter's daughter, Persephone.

The young girl just disappeared. Gathering flowers, "over a soft field," she fell into a trap. She reached for a peculiarly beautiful narcissus that Zeus had planted as a snare for her, and as she reached for it, Hades, the god of the underworld, grabbed her and bore her off in his chariot. Nor Hall's translation of the "Homeric Hymn to Demeter" describes that flower:

> It was a thing of awe whether for deathless gods or for mortal men to see; from its root grew a hundred blooms and it smelled most sweetly, so that all wide heaven above and the whole earth and the sea's salt swell laughed for joy. And the girl was amazed and reached out with both hands to take the lovely toy; but the wide-pathed earth yawned there in the plain of Nysa, and the lord, Host of Many, with his immortal horses sprang out upon her—the Son of Cronos, He who has many names.

For nine days Demeter, Persephone's mother, the great golden-haired goddess of the harvest, wandered over the earth, searching for her daughter. Fearing Zeus, no one told her where the girl was. But at dawn on the tenth day, "bright-coiffed" Hecate, who had heard the girl scream, met Demeter by torchlight and told her that she thought Persephone had been kidnapped, and that the sun god, Helios, had seen the whole thing happen. Yet when the two blonde goddesses found Helios, he told Demeter to "cease her loud lament." Helios didn't see a problem with the situation: From his point of view, Hades wasn't such a bad husband for Demeter's daughter.

Demeter covered her shining hair, and roamed the earth grieving for her daughter. She disguised herself as an old hag, and neglected her goddess duties. Crops withered and famine took hold. A year passed. Finally, Zeus, seeing this mess, made a deal with his brother to get Persephone back.

But Hades tricked Persephone into eating food in the underworld, and thus ensured that she would return to him for half the year, every year. And that explains why we have seasons. Winter begins when Persephone goes down to be with Hades, spring begins when she comes back to us.

As Hall remarks, the myth of Demeter and Persephone describes a draw in the battle between "father culture" and "mother culture," two different worldviews that were fighting it out just when the Homeric hymns were being written, in the seventh century B.C. The contract drawn up between Persephone's mother and Persephone's husband effectively split the young girl's life down the middle. But that contract hasn't held up too well over the centuries.

As the balance of cultural values tipped toward the masculine, with the reigns of Yahweh and Zeus, the myths of the people began to illustrate the demise of the power of the female. Demeter's anger was at her own powerlessness, at her own bereavement. The anger in my mother's eyes was not just at the vulgarity of it all. It was a reflection of Demeter's anger.

Persephone's wild ride in Hades' chariot signaled the end of her mother's ability to protect her. From the time of that kidnap, during which she called to her father and to all the gods for help and got no answer, she was on her own, surviving a situation she did not understand and could not control.

Every girl child crosses the chasm between mother culture and father culture sooner or later. I made the crossing wearing tape on my thighs while the birdlike James Bouffet whipped up the chariot's immortal horses. In every one of the last twenty-seven centuries, woman has strived to balance the demands of her female psyche and her male culture. In our era, this balancing act has taken an odd turn.

Today, our Persephones are lured by a different flower— our narcissus is made by Kodak. Our Innocent Blonde is amazed, and reaches out with both hands to take the lovely toy, but that toy is a photograph of herself. Our girl child is seduced by a father culture that offers her the dream of perfecting that photograph. She spends the rest of her life trying to resolve the difference between what she sees in her mirror and what she sees in the movies and in magazines.

As soon as she picks that flower, as soon as she is intrigued by her own image, the thundering chariot of father culture bears down upon her, and with it come a thousand rules and regulations about how she should look, and how she should act, and how she should be.

The first time she sees herself as a desired object, as a commodity, she becomes self-conscious and can be controlled by her own narcissism. It is in this strange chariot that she makes her first decisions about her own identity; it is during this wild ride that she often becomes a blonde.

Why are the modeling school mistress and the photographer and the stylist and the agent so often women? Why do women teach the rules and strictures of father culture? I suppose we shouldn't be surprised. The gulag archipelago, I am told, was built by its prisoners.

I, Defiler

I was about fourteen and Lita nineteen when it all happened. I prefer to think that the evening was nobody's fault. I am not a bitter person.

A few months before the experience, Lita shed her Marin hippie persona and swan-dived into sorority life in Berkeley. She was a strawberry blonde, a blonde, as Raymond Chandler once said, "to make a bishop kick a hole in a stained glass window."

I was learning to manage my newly sun-blonde hair for the first time, and modeling training lay fresh in my heart. Lita went off to Berkeley and was flirting her head off and eating Caesar salad and burgers at the Ratskeller while I remained behind in Terra Linda, reading Dag Hammarskjöld and wondering what cloudberries were.

But soon spring arrived—the spring of Persephone—and spring meant Russian Easter. Growing up half Southern Baptist and half Russian Orthodox made for the weaving of some heavy religious cabling in later life, but it was a fine thing when we were young. We got two of everything: two Christmases, two Easters.

As children, we looked forward to Russian Easter with great anticipation because it meant we would stay up all night. The idea of staying up all night was so grand, so impossibly romantic, that it obscured the religious significance of the midnight church service and the social significance of the family party afterward. In the early hours of the morning, we ate and ate and the men drank vodka toasts to the ladies, and we listened to the music that had been banned in our house during Lent. These parties often went on for days, people moving from house to house and from table to table.

American Easter meant coloring Easter eggs and eating a lovely dinner on the Indian Tree china, but Russian Easter was exciting, and simmered with an undercurrent of pagan release. It was rumored that some of the Orthodox husbands and wives didn't make love for the forty days and nights before Easter. This lent a special crackle to the atmosphere.

Every year my whole family gathered outside the church and devised a plan of attack about where to stand, for Russian Easter is so crowded that streets in front of Russian churches are generally blocked off and fire regulations completely disregarded. The idea was to try to be able to see what was going on in front.

What was going on in front was a commemoration of Christ's resurrection, and the service had not changed in any way since 1054 A.D. The Russians had an "If it ain't broke don't fix it" approach to religion for quite a few hundred years. Then, of course, they went at it with a machete, but that was a while ago now.

The night that it all happened the church was filled with clouds of incense, and priests sang antiphonal responses to the music of the huge choir. Sometimes two choirs sang back and forth, a children's choir and an adult choir, echoing and emphasizing each other's words. The children's choir held a number of my relatives, and they stood, wearing their light blue robes, to the side of the altar in the front of the church.

The music sounded burnished. Every phrase, every bow of the priests, had been repeated over and over for hundreds and hundreds of years, since the beginning of Orthodoxy, since the beginning of Russia.

No women participate in these rites, for women are not allowed behind the altar in the Orthodox church. The Orthodox believe in original sin, and hold Eve responsible for the downfall of Adam. Nevertheless, the Great Mother looks down upon most congregations from her frescoed place on the ceiling, right above the altar. The golden-haired Virgin—the "All-Holy, immaculate, most blessed and glorified Lady, Mother of God and Ever-Virgin Mary"—watches the priests chant. This is a bit of a discrepancy.

The altar in a Russian church is divided from the congregation by an iconostasis, a sort of freestanding wall with small doors that are painted with pictures of saints. In its middle, a large arch frames the altar itself. The entire iconostasis is decorated with frescoes and gold leaf, making its side doors invisible when they are closed. If you are standing in the congregation, one long phalanx of somber saints divides you from the altar.

At Easter, churchgoers of every stripe press together right up to the little stage in front of the iconostasis. The frail old rapid-genuflector in the pin-striped suit stands shoulder to shoulder with the loud-talking ex—Soviet atheist in the patchwork eelskin jacket. Suspicious old babas in kerchiefs patrol the candelabra, silently removing any candles that threaten to burn too low.

Once my family had made its annual plan of attack about where to stand, we eased into the crowded church one at a time. Taller than most, we regrouped in the back in a sort of grove of Ilyins. This was where the tough part of the evening began, for in Russian churches the congregation stands for the whole service. Standing for three unbroken hours during the Easter rites is not considered unusual.

My father was not about to torture himself or his children, so he cut our stand down to its bare minimum, an hour or so. But he could cut it no further, for we were surrounded by relatives and he didn't want them to think that being half WASP had weakened our blood.

We stood there in a candlelit group every year, my father slowly swaying back and forth imperceptibly to keep his blood moving, my sisters and me in a line from eldest to youngest, all holding candles. My mother, respectful, the nonparticipatory Protestant, at my father's side.

We never understood a word of what was being intoned and repeated. We did not speak Russian, and even the Russians didn't understand the Old Slavonic in which most of the service was conducted. I stood there year after year, and still stand there every year, feeling the warmth of the words wash over me, bowing slightly when the incense is shaken toward me, crossing myself when the memorized moment comes. For we all learned these things by rote, though we understood nothing of them.

On that particular night, my father, sisters, and I met to make our traditional standing plan of attack. But that Easter Lita and I had decided to beat the system. We had an inside source to great standing room, and we planned to use it.

Earlier that week, Lita and I had gotten together and made the *dernier cri* in fashionable evening attire. It was the year of the slip dress, aptly named, and so she and I made identical slip dresses for ourselves. Hers was violet. Mine was turquoise. My mother, who never blocked our fashion experiments, only insisted that we wear coats so as to maintain our modesty, for she understood our desire to take the family party by storm, and to dance around to Julio Iglesias's "Manuela" until the morning light.

That evening before church Lita and I donned our slip dresses and blew our blonde hair out huge, a radical step, for the smell of singed hair often went up around the congregation on Easter. Armed with prior knowledge of luxurious standing room, we threw caution out and doubled up on the spray. A bit of makeup and we were off.

A few days before, my cousin Marina had dropped by our

house for a cup of tea before she continued on to Fort Ross, where she was a summer guide. Marina was a churchgoer, and she spoke fluent Russian. She sang in the children's choir (some of the children being of a *certain age*), she knew the cathedral like a rat knows a ship, and she had an idea.

She told us about a quiet, peaceful little place next to where the children's choir stood, near the altar. It was a space in the shadow of a very large icon—I think it was a copy of Rublev's *Holy Trinity*—that stood on the left side of the little stage, right in front of the iconostasis.

"Go in the side door of the church," Marina had said, "go down the long hall, make a left, go up the little flight of stairs, and there's a door to the choir loft. Just go out the door. You'll be right by me—you'll be able to see everything, and you can stand behind the icon so no one will see you."

And so this was the plan that Lita and I proposed to carry out. We kept it to ourselves, for we didn't want anyone else horning in on our newfound territory. After taking our places in the Ilyin group for fifteen minutes or so, Lita and I edged our way back out the door, trying to look like helpless flotsam in the tide of humanity that was surging in. Once out, we minced to the little side door of the church in our stiletto strappy sandals, took a quick look left and right to see if we had been followed, went in, and pulled the door closed behind us.

It was black inside. We had candles but no match. Lita and I waited for our eyes to adjust. Slowly the black gave way to gray streaks at the far end of a long hall. We could hear the choir's singing slowly falling away as it followed the procession of priests out the doors and around the outside of the church. We wanted to get into our secret place while some of the congregation filed out and followed the procession. All were supposed to follow, but we knew that many old diehards would not leave their hard-won standing places. We knew we would have to be very quiet, because the church would still be full of silent people waiting for the stroke of midnight, the moment when the archbishop would knock on the huge doors to the church as if knocking on the door to Christ's tomb. We wanted to be in our place before the festive Easter hymn began, before the archbishop's first exclamation, "Christ has risen!," before the congregation's responding shout, "Truly He has risen!"

The great doors to the cathedral would then open and they would all come flooding in, coming to reclaim the deserted altar—all the priests and acolytes in dazzling white-and-silver robes, fresh white flowers bound to their censers. How grand it all would be from where we would stand.

We felt our way down the long hall, and made the left. The passageway seemed to be getting narrower, so narrow that the heat became intense, and Lita and I left our coats in a pile in a corner, to be picked up on the way back down.

Just as we were going up the little flight of stairs a priest suddenly shouldered toward us from out of nowhere, rushing in the other direction. We made way for him, not really knowing exactly what the etiquette was when you met a priest in a very narrow stairway in the dark. He said something curt in Russian as he rushed by, but neither of us understood it.

Somehow, in the bumbling with the priest, we lost our bearings. There was supposed to be a door to the choir loft—we were just supposed to go out the door. But there was no door. We felt around for a handle. All was silent. Outside, we could hear the procession singing, massing at the door to the church. "We're going to miss it," I hissed to Lita.

The next few moments were a bit confused. I don't remember whether Lita found a door handle and opened it aggressively, or whether I pushed her just a little in my rush not to miss the high point of the service. We jammed through the door and tumbled into a cool gray light.

We were in a very small room. A table stood in the center, and on it a gold reliquary, columned and spired like a small building. All was silent. Dark red curtains were closed across the front of the room. Behind them we heard the rustle of hundreds of waiting people. An old man coughed. A baby's wail drifted upward with the incense.

Directly above us, smiling her half smile, the Mother of God and Queen of Heaven looked down on us beatifically. It was just Lita and me and the Mother of God, the three of us, in the altar.

Suddenly priests in white robes were pulling back the red curtains, were moving around us everywhere, gesticulating at us wildly. The choir started its triumphant "Christ Has Risen" hymn while the perspiring conductor looked back at us in horror, arms frozen in the air. Lita and I took a few steps forward, unsure about where, exactly, to go. Tall, blonde, confused, clad only in the barest of slip dresses, we minced out of the altar.

The rest I have tried to forget. I remember trying to get

down off the little stage, but the church was so packed that we couldn't get down the stairs. I remember the looks of terror in the eyes of the priests. I remember wondering if they would wash down the altar in case we had touched it. I remember wondering for the first time just what was so bad about our being there.

We had been off by about only three saint doors. I made out Marina in the choir ten yards away, staring at us in horror and pointing hugely at the big icon of the Holy Trinity. Lita and I ran for it, like rabbits to cover.

Across the congregation I saw my father's face. He had a look, not angry or ashamed, but stunned. He had a "How the heck did *that* happen?" look. He is a good father.

We cowered behind the icon while Lita felt around and found a saint that opened, and then we scrambled out of the limelight and back into the darkness of the hallway behind the iconostasis.

I don't remember the party afterward. I don't remember whether we danced around to "Manuela." I've repressed the rest of the evening, the way you repress a bad car accident. But even now, so many years later, when I meet a San Francisco Russian, he'll often get a faraway look in his eyes and say, "Didn't I see you at Easter once, years ago . . . in church?"

o o o

The Christ is a mythically female sign. His message is communal—he preached love and forgiveness. He symbolizes the cycle of birth, death, and regeneration: He was born, he bled, he died, he rose again.

In the Renaissance, Italian painters started to paint Christ as a blond. His blondness showed his difference from the average churchgoer; his blondness showed his innocence, his purity. He became as blond as the sun, as blond as Apollo.

By 1400, Russian Orthodox icon painters were painting Christ with hair the color of red gold, marking his difference from the dark saints around him, marking his similarity to the ruling class of Varangian blonds.

When the French began to convert the Vikings to Christianity, they reworked Christ into a blond warrior-god, to show his similarity, not his difference. "See, he's just like you. He's blond, like you."

Father culture creates structures to contain mother culture. The images we have of Christ are images created by a patriarchy that wanted to contain and preserve the mystery we call the mythic female.

o o o

When I was eleven or so, I decided that I was an agnostic, having just learned the word. I marched into my parents' bedroom to inform my father right before we were supposed to go to somebody's christening. I stated that, since I was now an agnostic, I felt that I should be reprieved from the coming church event. We had just gotten our first television. I hated standing. These two facts were connected.

I remember how my father sat down on the side of the bed

after my announcement of agnosticism. He looked tired, and talked to me as though I were his age. He said, "There is form and there is content. You see what I mean, cuteso? This is a vase. You put water in the vase. How do you hold the water, without a vase? It's important to have a vase because then you have somewhere to put the water." As I said, he is a good father.

Sun Blonde

The first time I met Rita she was standing in the black shade under the overhang of her garage, watering our lawn with one hand, holding the one-year-old Linda on her hip with the other.

My father had just bought the house; she was our next-door neighbor on Las Gallinas Avenue. In Spanish, our new street's name meant "Avenue of the Hens." How true this turned out to be, for mostly the men were gone, working.

It was a blinding California midday in July—at least 100 humidity-free degrees. Our lawn would have been toast in two days had it not been for Rita. Her hair was up in curling papers. My father kissed her hand. She must have been in her late twenties.

Rita had grown up on a chicken ranch in Petaluma, her parents German immigrants from a place described to me as "The Isle of Fir." I never could understand how an isle could be a part of Germany. To this day I picture Grandma Ginna sailing away from a lake isle, like Innisfree with conifers.

Rita didn't know where The Isle of Fir was either. She was a Californian and didn't look back. She was more of a run-to-Sears, wash-the-Chrysler, and let's-take-the-kids-to-McDonald's type of gal. She saved my life, but that's another story.

Rita canned tomatoes in tomato season, beans in bean season, peaches in peach season. She introduced me to the philosophical concept of the chest freezer. She baked her apple pies in September, her fruitcakes at Christmas (not too many raisins, Fred did not like raisins), and her German cookies all year round. I particularly remember the labor-intensive tiny pastry shell filled with a white pastry cream, iced with a hardening chocolate glaze, and finished with a tiny kiss of the white filling in the center. It is my madeleine.

There were no dank corners in the lives of Rita and Fred. He worked at the bank, she ran the house. And run it she did, in a way never to be seen again in America. This was no mechanical bride. This was no tranquilized, alcoholic, over-educated-for-her-societal-role, undervalued, cast-aside, low-self-worth woman who'd rather be doing something else but got stuck with the short end of the stick. No. Rita was the last of her tribe. She was happy.

At our house, things were a bit confused. Soon after our arrival, my Southern grandmother began to slip slowly into

Alzheimer's in the living room, while my father's painting, formerly cheery and Impressionistic, went suddenly brown and grayish and began to drip. My mother was keeping an eye on both of them, but mentally she was working on the Venetian-style hat she was going to make out of that scrap of brown Brussels lace when she got a moment.

Nadia was married and gone, but my elder sister Lita was in the midst of the eschewing of bourgeois materialism that came to its truest fruiting in the sanctified groves of girls' private schools in the early seventies. She was also in the living room, studying French verbs. I did not notice my sister Anna at all, except when she bit.

The path I beat through the grass to Rita's soon became a permanent part of our landscaping. She taught me what to plant in a vegetable garden. She taught me crop rotation and rototilling. When I smell the acrid smell of tomato vines, I think of Rita. I remember her lugging boxes of zucchini over to our house—the two-foot kind of zucchini, the kind that hide until they're big enough to live in. Because of Rita, I developed a lifelong, and as yet unsatisfied desire for a sewing machine with a built-in buttonholer.

Once a month, Rita's sister came down from Petaluma. Wordlessly, the two of them put on rubber gloves and plastic caps. They shut themselves in the kitchen and performed what seemed to be a highly choreographed and much practiced dance, a dance punctuated by intermittent rings of the kitchen timer.

During these visits, I baby-sat and was curious. What were they doing in there? It seemed to involve chemistry. There was much mixing and holding-up-of-bottles. I suppose Rita thought I was too young to know that she was in there brushing up the lights.

Rita was from the naturalistic school of fake blondes. She kept her coloring quiet. In twenty-eight years, I've never seen her with dark roots. Her blue eyes fool you.

Rita was a self-taught blonde. She decided she wanted to be blonde because of something whispered in the advertising in *Good Housekeeping* and *Ladies' Home Journal,* something mumbled in the soaps, something assumed in the movies. She became blonde because blonde was all around her: at Safeway, at Long's Drugs, in the parking lots and drive-throughs of suburban California life.

I wanted that nice, normal family that gathered every night to watch TV and eat ice cream and pie. I wanted that chest freezer, that rototiller, that sewing machine. In short, I wanted to be like Rita, and so, when James Bouffet slumped with a plaintive cry, the blonde I chose to be was Rita's blonde, Summer Wheat Blonde.

Remember your boxes? The Summer Wheat Blonde is the second most popular blonde around. She symbolizes growth and rebirth and the goodness of grain: She is our mythic female nutritive.

In the old mythologies, earth goddesses romped about having sex and bearing children all the livelong day. But in America, we don't like to mix sex and motherhood. We like one to come before the other. So we divide this blonde's life into two distinct parts. When our Summer Wheat Blonde is young, she's working on her hearth and home skills, but when she's older, she becomes our blonde mother goddess.

This is the profile of a Young Summer Wheat Blonde: Her hair, or part of it, is the color of a corn tassel. She's direct, honest, and practical. She likes the idea of tofu, but can't give up pork chops. She plans on having children and likes to be around them. She knits interesting and textured wools into large and comfortable garments. She likes sex, but doesn't overthink it. Her future husband falls in love with her the day she turns up at his apartment unexpectedly, splits an avocado, fills it with sour cream and caviar, and pushes it toward him on a plate.

Unlike our Innocent, the Young Summer Wheat Blonde is not living in the enchanted garden of a never-ending childhood. The Greeks would have said she was not *kore* (girl) but *parthenos* (an unmarried young woman). Her Young Summer Wheat Blondeness often starts around fourteen, and ends when she has children, whereupon she becomes the Mature Summer Wheat Blonde. (At this point the Greeks would have given her their highest accolade for a woman, calling her *meter*—mother.)

The Mature Summer Wheat Blonde is bounty personified. Keats profiled her in his "To Autumn." She is a

> Season of mists and mellow fruitfulness,
> Close bosom-friend of the maturing sun,
> Conspiring with him how to load and bless
> With fruit the vines that round the thatch-eaves
>   run. . . .

She has easy labors and nice children. Her nurturing instincts blossom when she has kids: She buys a dehydrator and makes organic fruit roll-ups. She can fix the lawn mower. Men like her, are themselves with her. She is in tune with the rhythms of life and death. You often find her nursing, tending patients in the intensive care unit.

You know you are in the presence of a Mature Summer Wheat Blonde if the woman you are looking at has golden blonde in her hair, real breasts, full hips, and perhaps a tiny bit of a stomach; if she lives in a tousled house full of kids and dogs and half-finished sewing; if she shows up with hot tea and honey when you have a cold. Your massage therapist is a Summer Wheat Blonde.

Summer Wheat Blondes are not known for their great intellectuality. I don't remember Rita ever coming over and saying: "Here're your tomatoes, but just remember that physical objects are imperfect copies of their abstract forms." Smart and intellectual don't always share the same scooter. Anyone who has ever taken the physician's assistant boards in oncology has been surrounded by smart Summer Wheat Blondes.

At her least cerebral, the Summer Wheat Blonde thinks long and hard about becoming a Tupperware representative. At her most mythically evolved, she reflects the positive aspects of the Great Mother archetypal image, nurturing others through all the stages of life.

Illustrated manuscripts from the early Middle Ages often show a miniature of a blonde woman holding a sheaf of wheat or an ear of corn. Her robes are blue, her eyes are blue, her hair is painted in gold, the wheat is gold. She is Virgo, the astrological symbol for a constellation that reaches its highest point in the sky in late May, just in time for the growing season.

Virgo protected the harvest, watched over the birth of children, and looked after the cycle of growth, death, and regeneration. Her blonde hair represents the abundance and goodness of the wheat that she protects. But her hair color also reminds us of her own value, her own goodness, and her own purity. Her hair reminds us that she is the sun's coconspirator.

Virgo synthesized many of the attributes found in the ancient mother goddesses of Egypt, Babylonia, and Crete. These religions revered the creative force of nature, and their symbols took female form. Nature and woman seemed allied: Their cycles were both unexplained.

But isn't Virgo's virginity a little strange? After all, she's supposed to be having an affair with the sun. He passes through her constellation, bringing forth crops. She's got a lot of the ancient mother goddesses, who were no blushing brides themselves, in her. Why, then, the virginity?

Sarah Pomeroy tells us in her book *Goddesses, Whores, Wives, and Slaves* that in Greek myth, when a relationship between a goddess and her mortal followers was inspirational or protective, that goddess was often represented as a virgin. That's why the Greek goddesses Artemis (goddess of the countryside) and Athena (goddess of justice, wisdom, and warfare)—both blondes, incidentally—were virgins. Artemis was mostly inspirational and Athena was mostly protective. They had to be focused on the events in the lives of their mortal charges. They couldn't afford to be messing around. And so they were styled virgins to avoid all that running about after film teachers and so on.

In one sign, the golden-haired Virgin Mary brings together protection, inspiration, and fruitfulness. She's like Virgo, but she's a more complex image. The sun passed through the blonde Virgo once a year, but the godhead passed through Mary. These blonde mythic images fold in on themselves, taking in more meaning each time they reappear. They come to us many-layered, like golden puff pastry.

Finding a true Summer Wheat Blonde in the media these days is difficult because she is not thin and is not running around dating the crown prince of Monaco. She doesn't get a lot of press. But we do have one contemporary goddess who is her patron saint: the mother of all Summer Wheat Blondes, Martha Stewart.

Now, let me say right here that I have done my share of Martha Stewart bashing. When I was in graduate school, I was the most vociferous of bashers. I bashed for what I deemed ethical reasons.

At the beginning of her career, in the moneyed eighties, a young Martha Stewart taught an unwashed baby boom about how to make canapés and what to serve at a proper wedding. She promoted the value of home and hearth, showed pictures of casually-thrown-down brunches, championed time spent in pursuit of the perfect home.

The Martha Stewart who first appeared in the mediated pantheon was a woman who could do anything. She gathered her still warm eggs from her photogenic chickens, scraped the chipped paint off her own windowsills, and burnished her own heirloom silver. She staked peonies, served up suppers in wide ceramic bowls, ironed her antique linens, and baked three-layer cakes. Women flocked to buy her books. They were exhorted to slipcover their folding chairs in voile and hold festive blue-and-white clambakes by the sea. The magazine was born.

Martha seemed to work her magic completely on her own, and that's what irked me. There she was, organizing, painting, spackling, making tarts, growing herb topiary. But I knew one of her florists. I knew people who worked on her magazine. I knew she was commanding an army of professionals. I thought she was holding up an impossible dream to American women, making them feel worse than they already felt about their ability to hold it all together. But as it turned out, I was wrong.

○ ○ ○

One day an association asked me to give a big speech about the future of graphic design education. I blithely said yes, having no idea what the future held, and flew to Aspen, where they put me up in a luxurious off-season hotel. Provosts and deans showed up from all over the country. It dawned on me somewhere over Iowa that I would be speaking to one large group made up of all my potential future employers.

Now, in order to override my intense fear of public speaking, I have to fortify my ego to such an extent that it finally mows down all possibilities of failure, like a tank rolling over small trees. I spent the night before my speech walking up and down my lovely suite talking to myself and gesticulating deftly. I also ate a large room-service steak, courtesy of the association.

By the time I gave my speech the next morning I was floating on a cloud of adrenaline, protein, and hubris. The speech went well.

To celebrate, I went to the hotel hair salon and got a curvaceous blow-out, readying myself for the awards banquet that night. The kind association president seated me at his table, and introduced me to a number of distinguished midwestern provosts and their wives. My ego still fully inflated, I turned to speak with the sun-blonde-highlighted wife on my right, honoring her with my full attention.

She got started about the art of napkin folding, and wasn't this a lovely room and so on, and I don't remember who brought it up first, but Martha's name was mentioned. Suddenly I heard my own voice launching into a magnificent Martha-bashing monologue. And oh, I was hilarious. The irony about her having been a stockbroker in a former career. The satirical raised eyebrow about her divorce. The truth about her army of assistants, that she hadn't staked a sweet pea herself in ten years. The Polish-American middle-class background. Oh—the wit, the gestures, and, finally, through my fog of Self, the silence.

I looked around the table. All the women were giving me the hairy eyeball. One of the provosts coughed nervously. I looked at my dinner partner. She sat stiffly. And then she said, "Those may be the facts, but they're not the truth about Martha Stewart."

As it turned out, she was the president of the Milwaukee Martha Stewart fan club. Martha had been to her home. They had stuffed grape leaves under the skin of her holiday turkey together. I backtracked. I serpentined. I tap-danced. But it was of no use. I had blasphemed the goddess.

Since grad school, I had been waiting for the moment that American womanhood would realize it had been duped and would rally against Martha. But I hadn't realized that they already knew she was a fraud, and that they *did not care*.

When women worshiped at the statue of Diana, they didn't expect her to be like them. They expected her to protect them, to inspire them. The provost's wife loved Martha not for what she was, but for what she protected. Women across America breathed a sigh of relief when Martha came on the scene. Maybe they didn't have the time to sew weights into their tablecloth corners themselves, but Martha remembered how to do it, and that meant that the knowledge would not be lost, that the art of home would continue.

Nobody cared that Martha was not what she championed. So what that the husband had gone bye-bye? Martha had re-invented herself as a virgin mother, her child not so much a product of a union with a man but an assurance that the party would continue, and beautifully.

As she slowly came in from the cold, stopped pretending that she was gathering hen-warmed eggs herself, and took the reins of her multimedia empire, women loved her even more. And I learned a big lesson. As a preacher friend of mine says about himself, "They do as I say, not as I do, because I'm not the kind of man I'm preaching to."

Farrah and the Song Girls

Las Gallinas Avenue was put down by a contractor's pencil, and it cut straight through Terra Linda, our perfect grid of suburb. The street did not acknowledge its surroundings: The huge California sky and rough golden hills and southern view of Mount Tamalpais played no part in the developer's plan. We all knew the story of Tamalpa, the beautiful Miwok maiden who lay down one day and turned into earth and stone. But the raised ranches and tri-levels on Las Gallinas faced due east or west. We could not see the mountain, and our blank-faced houses stared, unblinking, at each other.

Las Gallinas sprouted little planned offshoots, like Vista del Mar, from which you could not see the sea, and Cherry Hill Lane, where no cherry trees grew. But if you walked up past the houses, the paving stopped and the street dwindled to a dirt track crossed only by the muffled deer trails that wound round the hill lightly and irrationally.

When we lived there, Las Gallinas Avenue did not teem with overt cultural diversity. In those days, sameness, not difference, was the goal. All was hammered into unity.

Rita's best friend, Doris, who lived across the street, brought Rita big flats of frozen ravioli. Were they Italian-American? Who knew? Rita always called her "Doris Across-the-Street." To me she was a splash of color and a friendly wave that existed in the world across the median strip.

Rita only evidenced her German background in her attraction to Hummel figurines. My friend Leslie, half Greek, knew no Greek, and my sisters and I spoke no Russian. My friend Claire was ethnically Jewish, now that I look back on it, but no one was exactly observing Yom Kippur over there. I think some black people lived in the house with the abundant azaleas, but I never saw them.

The people who moved to Las Gallinas Avenue came there without a past, and lived like stateless people. They came with no history, and made none.

In New York people routinely call you up and say things like "Come on over! My sister's here with her Serbian boyfriend, and our neighbors are going to drop by—you remember them—she's Ashkenazi and he's Sephardic." But when I was growing up in California, everyone in my white-bread suburb was making an effort to be identical.

When everyone is different, the pointing out of difference is merely description. But when everyone is trying to look the same, the pointing out of difference has the ring of prejudice. Once, when my European brother-in-law described some friend of his as a second-generation Hungarian, I remember thinking, "Aren't we beyond that yet?" as if it were only a matter of time until the entire country would develop cultural amnesia, and what a good thing that would be.

Since no one in the suburbs acknowledged a cultural heritage, we were on our own when it came to making up the stories that bind a community together. It was up to us to make up some sort of mythology, our own mythic tools and symbols, our own gods and goddesses, our own prodigious trials and accomplishments. We were the most primitive of societies, alone as we were, together. It was like *Lord of the Flies* with Lifebuoy.

In California, we were cast adrift, inhabiting houses on a raw land that was ready to buck us at the first opportunity. The tidy green of our lawns stood in ephemeral contrast to the dun of the hill grass. I remember looking up, out of the upstairs window as evening fell, looking at the black silhouette of the houses lined up on the hillcrest. They looked like a line of covered wagons circled for the night against a hostile enemy. We were interlopers, and we felt it.

Where did we turn to find our mythic stories? Well, like all Americans in all suburbs, we had television to guide us with some of the larger gods. The rest we made up as we went along. At Terra Linda High, the Committee on Traditions met twice a year, and cobbled together an ad hoc mythological system that suited the needs of the people.

They named our football team the Trojans. Like the condom. I couldn't make this up. They went whole hog for poetic consonance without considering popular culture: "The Terra Linda Trojans." The mental image was just too happily phallocentric, and the PTA's annual attempts to change the name on the grounds of delicacy were warded off by the administrative patriarchate.

The larger ramifications of what it meant to be a Trojan (stealing the blonde Helen, losing the war after being tricked by the Greeks, the dead Hector being dragged around the walls in the dust, Aeneas escaping the flames with his blind father on his back, and so on) were not given any thought because our vulgate mythology stopped short of book learning. In a bizarre twist, we often rode a huge Trojan horse float on spirit days, which is mythically equivalent to the Japanese riding a big raffia-papered atomic bomb float in the Rose Bowl parade.

After it has established its turf and its defense system (in our case symbolized by the high school football team), the first thing a primitive society needs is the assurance that it will keep going. Consequently, my suburb, along with many, many other suburbs, adopted a contemporary fertility goddess: the California Sun Blonde.

The California Sun Blonde is the most photogenic of the sun-wheat-and-growth blondes. She substitutes water for grain, and often stands in front of ocean waves, her hair mist-lifted by the salt spray. She generally wears a bikini, whether it is fashionable or not, so that you can see as much of her body as possible, and so that your attention will be particularly drawn to those parts that are covered. She often holds a huge surfboard, the *ne plus ultra* of contemporary phallic symbols.

Water and oceans often symbolize sex and freedom in dream analysis—we crawled out of the sea, it was our first womb. The uncontrolled ocean rolls free—except for the pull of the moon. The rhythms of the lunar cycle correspond to the rhythms of a woman's body. That California Sun Blonde standing on a golden beach is the connecting point for sand, sun, and sea.

Cheerleading is the natural vocation for a California Sun Blonde. She spends a lot of time jumping up and down outside in the sun, rehearsing. All my friends became one sort of cheerleader or another. This began our great divide. By sophomore year, I was taking my first stabs at establishing a languidly arrogant persona, and began carrying around *L'Étranger*. I stood about the halls of the English department and tried to look like I was in thought. This behavior was tolerated awfully well by my cheerleading friends, but the boisterous parade of Trojan spirit had passed out of sight by junior year, leaving me to wander the mocking, empty halls alone.

o o o

You know you're in the presence of a California Sun Blonde if she has never left, or wishes she could return to, the state of California. She has a tan, real or sprayed on. She wears shorts in February. She rehearses the arm movements to cheerleading routines while waiting for you in the parking lot. When she matures, she often takes on Mature Summer Wheat Blonde coloration. But, with her tan and her shorts and her sunglasses, she remains our beachy sun goddess.

In the ancient mythologies, there is no "sun goddess" per se. The fertility goddess is an earth goddess; she is about the dark and generative powers of the life force. She usually exists in tandem with a sun god; she is often his lover as well as his sister. The sun god's warmth and light inspires the new life to which the earth goddess gives birth. She is made fertile by his warmth. In pictures, when the earth goddess is symbolized by a blonde, her hair color reflects her intimacy with the sun god.

We Americans reinvented and exported this goddess. We had the beach, the blondes, and the cameras. We made movies, and pushed the California Sun Blonde around the globe from the time silent movies caught her running in from the ocean in her knee-length swimsuit. Our blonde earth goddess still runs along the beach in *Baywatch*.

We make sure the world listens to our story of blonde by running her up and down that beach over and over and over until everybody gets it, from Pakistan to Peru. Think of what this does to global culture. Think of what it does to you.

Back on Las Gallinas, we sprayed on the Sun-In and tried to look as though we could be running around with surfboards. But Terra Linda is an hour from any beach, and when you finally did get to one, the fog was so thick and the brown sand so damp that you retreated at once to an inn to warm up by a crackling fire with some hot apple cider. Of such is northern California beach culture.

Nevertheless, we tanned in the backyard, wearing our faux Hawaiian print string bikinis, smoothing on the cocoa butter. California Sun Blondes are cheery by nature, so we all talked the same way, cultivating a breezy, hopeful tone, a tone later imitated perfectly by Moon Zappa.

When I was in high school, still a time of wide-leg hip huggers and headbands, cheerleaders dressed in archaic garb. This was expected. They set their hair, something that had not been seen in real life since the early sixties. They wore little tummy-taming panty girdles under their kick pants at a time when the news was carrying pictures of bra burnings. They wore suntan-colored tights and little white Keds, which were completely out of style. They wore what had been fashionable when the high school had first been built, when the Committee on Traditions had met for the first time.

These were the hippest girls in the school, and when they took on the title of cheerleader, or "Song Girl," as we called them, they accepted teased hair and kick pants as part of their heritage. And we accepted their curls and their panty girdles because they were acknowledged higher beings: They were popular, they were pretty, and they could dance their heads off in those little white Keds.

We worshiped them. There they were, at every game, bobbing alongside the football team, live female totems of growth and continuance, a line of Venuses reassuring the young Trojan warrior that sex and procreation were conveniently located nearby. These were our cultish fertility goddesses, our home-grown deities. They, in turn, looked to an even greater goddess.

From the time she was about eight, Rita's daughter Linda had a big, signed poster of this goddess in her bedroom, and when I baby-sat, Farrah Fawcett smiled down upon us, her leonine hair thrown back, her huge smile dominating the room, her burgundy swimsuit the color, a mythologist would say, of menstrual blood. She was the goddess our cheerleaders imitated, she was the one they wanted to be like, the blonde earth goddess for whom they danced their mystery dance.

Farrah and the Song Girls were a cleaned-up expression of mother culture, an expression of something not on top in human consciousness since father culture had come in with Hesiod and Homer. Yes, their perfect bodies made them desirable to the boys and to the fathers, and we'll get to that. But their cultural function went deeper, and the story they tell is a story that was told before the domination of the mythic masculine—before the reigns of Zeus and Yahweh.

The power of the cheerleaders came not from their individuality, but from their similarity. When they did their synchronized dance-and-pom-pom routines in the gym on game days, they danced to Motown tunes, they danced to the sound of the marching band. They shared the mesmerizing power of the Rockettes, of a chorus line or the Folies Bergère. Some people would say that they were all lined up there so that men could look at them, and that's true. But, deeper, theirs was a celebration, not of individuality, which is mythically male, but of repetition, which is mythically female. "I am that which is, has been, and shall be," reads the inscription on a Greek statue of Isis. "My veil no one has lifted. The fruit I bore was the Sun."

Your female side is the side that reminds you that the process of life actually has no goal. Life is creation, development, and repetition. Your female side sees a life in which babies are born and people die without much thought to the individual. This side is soothed by rhythm—the rhythm of ocean surf, of seasons, of music. This female side likes to see bridesmaids all wear the same dress.

Which brings us to pigs. The mythological symbol of the white sow is an ancient sign for that repetitive female urge, a sign of the raw power of rebirth. And yet, these days, when you happen to catch your rear view in the bathroom mirror while you're bent double taking the laundry out of the hamper, what do you call yourself? What do you chorus with the 30 million other women bent double across America cleaning out the hamper at that exact moment? "You pig! You big, fat, good-for-nothing pig." Or words to that effect. Strange that we choose this particular epithet to pound ourselves.

In *The Goddesses and Gods of Old Europe, 6500–3500 B.C.*, Marija Gimbutas tells us that the (big fat) pig was the sacred animal of the goddess of vegetation as far back as the Neolithic era, that is, as far back as we can trace any of humankind's created images. Sculptures of pigs crop up in archaeological digs all over Europe with the same frequency as sculptures of dogs, bulls, and he-goats. In other words, male and female are balanced off in ancient artifacts. The fast-growing body of the pig impressed ancient agricultural peoples, its fattening was compared to corn growing and ripening, and its fat came to symbolize the earth itself.

Demeter, the bare-breasted queen of corn, bread giver, and queen of the dead (manifested as her daughter, the aforementioned Persephone), is connected with the prehistoric vegetation goddess through her association with that big, fat, white pig.

Demeter's daughter Persephone was called "Pherrephata,"

"killer of little pigs," an unfortunate nickname given to her because of a nauseating Athenian rite in her honor in which (easy barfers stop reading here) women threw rotten suckling pigs onto the altars of Demeter and Persephone, and then mixed these carcasses with seeds to be used for that year's sowing.

Our culture is scared by big, fat pigs, scared by litters and blood and afterbirth and the whole messy, out-of-control business of birth, death, and regeneration. We live in a society that favors the left side of the brain, favors the logical, the scientific, the compulsive. Ours is the era of feminine hygiene. I still await my chance to pour the little glass beaker of blue liquid on the crisp white pad.

But deeply mythological signs have a way of sneaking down the fluorescent hallways of the media and appearing unannounced. Demeter's white sow came down that hallway on little tippy toes. The word "Farrah" echoes the word "farrow," a litter of pigs, from the old English word *fearh,* or "little pig," from the Greek *pherre.* What a symbol of fertility our Farrah was in the seventies! But she never knew that her name made reference to the corn-haired goddess's beautiful, mystical, big, fat pig.

Apollo in Drag

I enjoy flattery, and will elbow my way across a verbal no-man's-land to get it. My need for compliments is innate, for I come from a flattery background. My mother was partial to the Southern Openwork Approach ("You are a *charmin'* man!") while my father favored the Urbane Diplomatic Mode (eye contact over the kissed hand). For this reason, life at our house on Las Gallinas had a certain *Gone With the Wind* meets *Doctor Zhivago* quality, and there was much delighted noticing of small things.

Unfortunately, flattery is not in style in New York, and compliments here are suspect and openly spurned. There is a certain kind of New Yorker who believes that, in the continuing search for honesty in the man-woman relationship, a compliment is but a manipulative and underhanded attempt at control and domination. ("I know you're just saying that about my socks to get me to like you so that you can dump me after you've made yourself feel better by getting me to like you.") This attitude dries out a relationship faster than poison dessicates a mouse, and more than once I have been left, a dry husk of my former self, embedded in the insulation.

But I persist. And if people don't have a naturally complimentary nature, I manipulate, control, and dominate them into it underhandedly. So it was that I poked and prodded a recent romantic acquaintance into telling me just how good-looking I really was. After I had him in a verbal corner and he could do nothing but say something flattering, he cheerily proclaimed, "You're prettier than Miss Rhode Island, Natalia, but you're no Claudia Schiffer."

Now no woman with incipient crepe-neck really needs to ever hear about Claudia Schiffer, especially when that woman is craving something along the lines of "You are the single most gorgeous person I have ever seen and you are only becoming more beautiful as your face develops character." So I found it tough to metabolize this particular comment, especially the Miss Rhode Island part. We all have our own special way of neutralizing an offhand brutality. Some women claw, some weep, some harangue. I publish.

What kind of a mind visualizes a long tape measure that has Claudia Schiffer standing at one end and Miss Rhode Island (a really very lovely girl) standing at the other? What kind of mind looks at a woman and says to itself, "That left eyebrow definitely brings her down a notch in my book"?

Where does our fetish for measurement come from? How do we decide that one person is more good-looking (and therefore "better") than another? Why do comments made about our fat go to our bone? What happened along the way that made size six beautiful and size twenty a crisis?

Measurement is the apparatus of mankind's search for perfection. We hear all our lives about the "perfect body," "perfect proportion," "perfect features." But what does perfect mean, really? Where do we get the idea of "perfect"?

Well, Plato believed that a perfect "idea" exists outside our everyday life of real things. The "idea of tomato" is the archetypal most perfect of perfect tomatoes, perfect beyond comprehension, and our everyday tomato never measures up. None of our tomatoes is ever perfect, though they all participate in the archetypal Idea of Tomato.

The god Apollo was the Greek way of symbolizing a striving for that perfection. Apollo was originally the ancient Greek guardian of flocks and folds. Through the ages he merged with Phoebus, the god of light, and became Phoebus Apollo. After the fifth century B.C. he also took over the identity of Helios, the sun god. So there he was, a nice big god after all those mergers, all sun and light.

Remember learning about saturated solutions in chemistry? You put a string in a beaker and crystals developed along the string. Well, that's what a society does when it invents a god. A god or a goddess is an accretion of ideas, a big, complex symbol of the values of a culture crystallized into the recognizable shape of a human being. All those values are easier to remember and to respond to when we think of them as a person.

Apollo was the place where the Greeks put all their belief about the light of the mind—all their ideas of genius. Apollo was the lightbulb god, the "Aha!" god. And so he became the god you invoked when you made music, practiced medicine, played around with mathematics, composed poetry, sent an arrow into a target, or prophesied about the future. If there was inspiration in it, Apollo was there.

After the Dorians—a light-haired people from the north—got through with him, Apollo had become a beautiful blond youth. His image was a road map for perfection. And so we learned to measure and compare because the Greeks decided that one proportion was more beautiful than another, and because they thought that what you looked like on the outside reported what you were on the inside.

Classic proportions and long limbs meant beautiful bodies: They measured up, they looked like architecture. A beautiful body meant a beautiful soul. Your blond hair meant that the purity of the sun lived within you. Apollo's blond symbolized the beauty of the power that could order and control nature. It symbolized the beauty of the rational mind.

Now you notice we're talking blond, not blonde. This blond of Apollo is a male blond. (The Greeks were into male blonding.) You don't see women here because human perfection, to the Greek mind, meant male perfection. Sure, Aphrodite was quite the looker and good for a few laps, but if you were seriously searching for mental beauty and physical beauty in their most perfect combination, to the Greek way of thinking you were looking at the body and mind of a man.

Artists since the Renaissance have looked to Greek statues

for the okay on what is beautiful. What size should a head be? How long should a leg be? Greek proportions were copied laboriously by all art students up until the turn of the century. The people who copied those statues were the teachers of the teachers who taught us art history. Objects in the mirror are closer than they appear. These values have been handed down to us.

You can't speak a language, balance your checkbook, turn on the radio, take an aspirin, buy a Hallmark card, or read your horoscope without stumbling into the Apollonian in our culture. And there's not a woman in America who does not compare herself to the Apollonian ideal. We created our most, most favorite blonde goddess—the "sun-gold-and-purity" blonde—in his image. Apollo Blonde takes up more than half the blonde shelf space in your drugstore.

But he was a male god. Why would a woman want to imitate Apollo? Well. First remember that we're all made up of those male and female sides. And the male side of our American mind just loves the Apollonian, the dream of measurable beauty. So a woman has an innate drive toward "the perfect" within herself. But she is also living in a culture that is male side dominant. And since our male side is running things, it likes to see perfect images of itself.

In Greece, the cult of Apollo was homoerotic. Men loved the idea of the perfect man, literally. But since the Judeo-Christian ethic doesn't exactly embrace the idea of men standing about gazing at each other's perfect proportions, this admiration for Apollo has gone underground in our culture. The blonde you see on the cover of *Shape* magazine is Apollo in drag.

The Apollo Blonde is our cool sun blonde, the cool blonde of winter—pure, direct, like light on the Matterhorn. There is nothing Dionysian or chthonic about her. She is not a fertility goddess or a mother goddess, like the Summer Wheat Blonde, even though we veneer our cheerleaders with her perfection. Apollo Blonde is the blonde most of us want to be because she is so loved by the media. Men think she's attractive because her mind-set is not entirely foreign to them.

In her research into the lives of women in classical antiquity, Sarah Pomeroy suggests that the very fact of Athena's asexuality provides the reason for her constructive and friendly relationships with most of the major Greek heroes. There she was, giving advice and a friendly hand when you happened to need one on the battlefield. You didn't hear Achilles saying, "That Athena, she's such a *girl.*" No, she was a partner, a sort of calming psychic presence, a chance to regroup.

And so it is with our Apollo Blonde. She does not reek of sexuality. Instead of being about procreation and intense femaleness, she is a cultural projection of the perfect partner.

Now don't write to me and say that I've accused you of being asexual when it is so very clear that you enjoy being a girl. Relax. No one is insinuating that you don't love your pets, look after your children, or bake a luscious brownie. I've spent half my adult life trying to be an Apollo Blonde, so I'm taking myself down with you here. No one woman is entirely a type. I'm sure you're very sexy when you put your mind to it.

It is just interesting, isn't it, that the blonde we represent in the media is so very mythically male, so little mythically female?

Very few women are true Apollonians because the physical requirements are so unusual. Most of us fake it. We would be this sun blonde if we could, because she's all over movies, TV, bus shelters. She represents all we can buy, all we can achieve in a consumer culture. But why is she the blonde advertisers picked to popularize their products?

o o o

If the woman you are looking at has hair the pale gold of winter sunlight, if she is tall, tanned, has perfect, photogenic features, narrowish hips, not much waist, breasts only if implanted—if she is athletic and amazingly low in body fat, she's an Apollo Blonde.

She's often a trophy wife, a blonde of affluence, an armpiece. Her second house is in Sun Valley. She skis, she rides, she swims. She is a supermodel, the wife of a politician, a doctor, an architect. She keeps a journal, and prefers Mozart to Rachmaninoff. She does Pilates.

She thinks things through, is not stirred by a sudden whim or passion. Her children look just like her. She gets straight to the point—like Apollo's arrow to its target: You'll know it if she doesn't like your tie.

An Apollo Blonde will not drift into loving you without thinking. If she does have a relationship with you, it will be for a good reason. That reason may be your charm or your casual good looks, but it also may be your money, your social position, or your success in the arts or in politics.

The Apollo Blonde is not a hypocrite. If you ask her why

she married you, she'll tell you. So be careful. She is all sun, not earth. When mature, she often plunges into supporting the arts. When she works for money, she's the director of the ballet, a fund-raiser for the opera. When she works for charity, she teaches kids to read. (Reading is the mastery of a hierarchical system of signs—hierarchical systems, such as language, are Apollo's area.)

At their lowest intellectual ebb, Apollo Blondes can be shameless social climbers. They can be acquisitive, materialistic, cool-hearted, and unkind. But there's nothing like an evolved Apollo Blonde. The greatest Apollo Blondes inspire us. They are natural speakers, can frame an argument, and have educated minds. They use their intellectual gifts for the good of the culture, and often follow in Apollo's first calling, caring for flock and fold. She's the blonde who leaves her hard-earned partnership in the law firm to become a minister.

Most of the blondes you see in the media are Apollo Blondes, or are doing their best imitation. Let's see—well, in order of appearance in the two magazines currently lying on my bathroom floor, we have: Cameron Diaz; Marie Gray (the St. John knits gal); Patricia Arquette; Trudie Styler; Gretchen Mol; Lulu Johnson; Stacey McKenzie; Carolina Herrera; Kirsty Hume; Carolyn Murphy; Gwyneth Paltrow; Amber Valletta; Nicole Kidman; Bridget Hall; the aforementioned Claudia Schiffer; Pia Getty; Uma Thurman; Carolyn Bessette Kennedy; Alex Kuczynski; Annette Tapert; Anne Heche (worth an article in herself); Alexandra Von Furstenberg; Laura Dern; Sharon Stone; Jaime Rishar; Meg Ryan; Rene (highlights) Russo; Melanie Ward; Gabriele Sanders; Moyra

Mulholland; Jade; Eva Herzigova; Peggy Lipton; the contemporary Farrah, Diane Sawyer; Slim Keith; Lauren Bacall; Willow Bay; Peta Wilson; and Jeri Ryan. That's just two magazines. Think how many Apollo Blondes you've seen in a lifetime.

Youth is an important aspect of Apollo Blonde, for the god himself was imagined to be caught eternally at the moment of his full flowering. Most of the blondes I just listed are fairly young, or are remembered as young in photographs. Unlike Summer Wheat Blondes, who go through a maturing cycle, this blonde achieves her "look" at, say, fourteen—and keeps it, unchanged, till she drops in the traces.

Consequently, Botox, collagen, nips, tucks, and, finally, total and complete overhaul and renovation can be part of the Apollo Blonde's cosmetic kit. It's her way of ordering and controlling nature.

The Apollo Blonde is the blonde advertisers picked to popularize because she is so difficult to imitate. In order to close the gap between what I see in the mirror and the Apollo Blonde I see in a magazine, I'd have to shear off twenty pounds, invest in a neck strap, hit the gym every day, hire two trainers and a ball boy, and pick out a closetful of new clothes. All this costs money.

When was the last time you saw a Gap window and said, "Hey, I look *just like* that gal in the skimpy tee!" No, you scuttled off home feeling like a heel. And you bought something to make yourself feel better. Perhaps a recipe book for diet shakes, perhaps the large Kit Kat bar. You bought something because Ms. Apollo in the Gap window reminded you of how you don't measure up. A crevasse has opened up in your mind between the "you" that is you and the "you" you think you should be, and the thin end of the advertising wedge that created that crevasse is the Apollo Blonde. Perhaps that's why they call it the Gap.

We still believe that what we look like on the outside reflects what we are on the inside. This is our Greek legacy, and it fits in very nicely with our "buying" culture. Our economy depends on our feeling like toads. If you liked your wonderful Self all that much, would you go out and buy that "age-defying lotion," the new blow dryer with "frizz-ease styling wand," that "under-eye corrective concealer"? Of course not. The American economy would come to a Bugs Bunny, heel-screeching stop if tomorrow every woman in the country woke up, took a look in the mirror, wrapped her arms around herself, and said, "I just love good old me."

Apollo Blonde is consumerism's pal. Since she occurs so rarely in the genetic mix, she represents the perfect unattainable. Although she was invented by the Greeks, it is her rare appearance in real life that makes her attractive to advertisers. If wide hips occurred as infrequently in the gene pool, you can bet we'd all be wearing padded slips.

The Armpiece Years

My mother first heard the news from an acquaintance, not her favorite mode of informational transfer. The practiced eyes of the hostess smiled over the silver service. "I hear Natalia is seeing a *celebrity*."

Now, in some circles, "seeing a celebrity" is the adult version of being chosen prom queen. Given the chance, many mothers might have displayed an autographed picture of the celebrity prominently, perhaps over the fireplace in the family room. His videos would have lain upon the cocktail table, his books upon the shelf. My mother lived on a street of such family rooms. Yet these were not her sentiments.

Privacy was my mother's great luxury, and the preservation of privacy her great commitment. In those days I couldn't understand why anyone would want to avoid getting herself splashed all over *W.* But now I think I know why.

The armpiece venture came as a shock to my mother, because the last time she had looked, I had been padding along in soft shoes doing the hair-in-a-bun thing, teaching semiotics quietly at an excellent small institution. Teaching wasn't exactly what she had had in mind—I believe she had wanted me to marry a nice diplomat posted in a convenient European location. But she thought I had found my métier and was happy.

Being an adjunct professor should have been enough for me. But something in my heart still yearned for the klieg lights, longed for French twists and dinner suits, thought lustfully of Prada sling backs. And so it was that an umbrella strobe went off in my brain the day an old school acquaintance happened to say, "*You've* seen my father on TV, he's . . ." And through a series of shrewdly orchestrated, seemingly coincidental events—imagine! One day we bumped into each other, out of the blue, just like that.

I admit it was a course change. My mother, once the shock subsided, handled the whole thing with the delicacy of a plastic surgeon. She put a good face on it. I would mature from the experience. It would blow over. But it was a while before she could smell Earl Grey again without seeing that nauseating mental image of my feeding grapes to the toga-clad staff of *People* magazine.

Now let me say right here that my celebrity was a particularly good kind of celebrity, for he was celebrated only in certain circles. It wasn't like dating Al Pacino or anything. He was a nice, sedate kind of celebrity, just charming, and I would still be his armpiece today if it weren't for my facial neuralgia.

The doctor says that it happens sometimes. Years of smiling while clenching the teeth can destroy the trigeminal nerve. I had to retire early from being an armpiece, and it's too bad, too, for I had gotten quite used to my life as an Apollo Blonde.

When he first looked at me, my celebrity saw tallness, blondeness, and an innate knowledge of appropriate forks. When I looked at him, I saw the gateway to Paradise—dancing at charity balls, Norwegian cocktail parties on schooners, martinis at the Four Seasons, planked salmon on the terrace with a few friends, caviar and Champagne at Petrossian. Before I knew it, I was dancing, schoonering, besotted, and planked. This should have been a warning to me of my unfitness for the role: Besottedness is not Apollonian.

My formerly summer-wheat-and-air-dried hair became a controlled pageboy the color of cool sunlight. I was tall, but had to fake the athletic requirement, for I am as lazy as a snail and don't even climb stairs. To cover, I stood about country clubs wearing tennis sweaters tied around my neck and sunglasses on my head.

Body fat was a problem. Not a true Apollonian, I never could affect the breeze-into-the-Connecticut-living-room-in-riding-jodhpurs look because a) I fill out jodhpurs, and b) I can't ride a horse. Which reminds me of the time my young refugee Russian grandmother stood around a posh spa for three days wearing a tennis ensemble complete with racquet, though she didn't play tennis, because she couldn't afford any other clothes. But I digress.

I did not ride. I did not ski. My suburban girlhood really let me down in the area of active leisure-time skills. When I had leisure time on Las Gallinas, I usually sat out in the backyard and watched my beans grow. This well-honed ability did not prove very useful in the armpiece years.

My original technique for skiing avoidance was simple: I kept moving about the lodge. People thought I'd "gone up the mountain" when I was actually reading *Allure* under the stairs.

But, a word of warning if you're planning on becoming a non-skiing Apollonian Blonde—sooner or later all that faux après-ski lounging is going to back up on you, and your celebrity and a few dozen other ex–professional skiers are going to get you in a merry headlock and drag you up to an expert run. There is going to be no way out.

The first time this happened to me I found myself at the top of a craggy peak at the Whistler Resort in Canada. After leaping off the chairlift self-assuredly, I fooled with my ski as they all launched themselves nimbly down the run.

There we were: the empty chairlift, the whistling wind, the mountain crag, and me. I looked down the run. Sure death. At a loss, I pitched myself forward in the snow and begged the blue dome above for mercy. As luck would have it, seeing me tumble over, a guy who happened to be checking the lift cable came running over and asked me if I was all right. I did what any non-skiing Apollonian imitator would have done. I said I was pregnant.

We hung out and had instant hot chocolate in a little hut, and I learned all about chairlift mechanisms, and after much smiling and trigeminal clenching he took me back down on some sort of a snow scootery thing, and I ordered a cheeseburger from room service and took a nice bath just to quiet my nerves.

o o o

As an armpiece, I basked in luxury. This was a switch for the woman who once wrote a cookbook called *Ways with Lentils*. Sure, I still plodded along, a sober wage earner by day. But my nights were filled with chefs making chicken in Champagne sauce just for me because some silly person had taken it off the menu, like a fool, and we wouldn't want mademoiselle to be disappointed.

It was at one of these dinners that I looked keenly around the assembled group and realized that the women, all blondes, divided neatly into two groups: Armpiece Blondes and Trophy Blondes.

Armpiece Blondes and Trophy Blondes are not to be confused with Arm Candy, a current term for the blonde you don't know who walks you into the Oscars and gives people the impression that your life holds more than contract negotiations, calls to your broker, and takeout from Panaang.

No, the women I was looking at hold career positions. Armpiece Blondes and Trophy Blondes are two very different breeds of blonde, and you should know the difference. Like the verbs "to lay" and "to lie," you use them in completely different ways but they look identical in certain inflections.

A Trophy Blonde is primarily a visual object, and must be physically perfect in every way. If you are thinking of applying for this position, let me remind you that it is a career with a short life span. The average Trophy life is about three years, depending on how her skin holds up. Upon the inception of her third social season, the Trophy either announces her incipient breakup or makes it known that she is becoming an Armpiece by chairing her first charity event. This transition is difficult and not often achieved.

An Armpiece Blonde, on the other hand, is only secondarily a visual object. Yes, she must hone closely to Apollo standards, she must be good-looking, but she is not always—say—a Claudia Schiffer. Her great role, and value, is her deployment of her considerable mental gifts in the service of the career of her celebrity. She is a great listener, she remembers what the producer next to her said at dinner. She probes for details about the upcoming election. She charms the new secretary general. She helps.

Trophies can achieve Armpiecehood, but this is very rare. Trophy Blondes tend to turn the mirror inward. Armpiece Blondes turn it outward to reflect the smiling faces of other people. Suha Arafat is an Armpiece. Hillary tried. She really tried.

The Young Trophy talks a blue streak—about what her celebrity bought her, where they are going over the holidays, what she thought of his former wife. The Mature Trophy doesn't talk because talking stretches the skin. When the Young Trophy seems to be listening, she's really thinking about what she'll say next. When the Mature Trophy seems to be listening, she is really trying to remember the name of that liposuction clinic in Geneva.

The Armpiece listens acutely, remembering everything said.

She'll be ready for the debriefing in the car on the way home. She'll have come to a conclusion about the general political or economic situation by the time she puts her earrings on the bedside table.

Trophies don't laugh often, for laughter stretches the skin. The Armpiece laughs well, at other people's jokes.

o o o

Although my days of being an Armpiece are over, I have compiled a few thoughts for the woman thinking of a career move in this direction. First, the photographs.

As an Armpiece, it is of the utmost importance that you provide a sort of lambent glow around your celebrity at all photo opportunities. For this reason, you will master the Rear Lapping Deltoid Hug, in which you stand a few inches behind and lapping the celebrity, with your lapping arm laid upon his middle back in a gesture that can be interpreted as either consoling or supportive—as the need arises—but never looks clingy or intimate.

If taller than your celebrity, you will incline your smiling blonde head to the right or left in order to mask the disparity. For, though he dates you because you are tall as well as blonde, no man wants to look like a stump in the newspaper.

Certain committed long-term tall blonde Armpieces paired with short men have mastered the you-just-caught-me-sitting-on-the-fence-rail-while-he-leans-up-against-it-in-his-Stetson-on-our-huge-ranch pose, but this is really postdoctoral. For all other concerns about height conflicts, watch Nancy Kissinger.

For "live on tape interviews," and videoed occasions, it is particularly important for you to keep totally silent while smiling slightly and beaming a quiet approval at the celebrity while he speaks. Producers value clean tape, and you will seriously diminish your celebrity's chances of getting on the evening news if you screw up the sound bite. No one wants to hear the blonde talk.

One of the Armpiece's crucial tasks is to be the person people talk to when they don't have the nerve to talk to the celebrity himself. Whether in a receiving line, at a football game, or waiting in line to buy a roast, the Armpiece must be ready at all times to listen to hastily sketched-out plans and schemes that feature her celebrity as the "man-who-makes-the-pitch-to-the-public." The adoption of a well-rehearsed, slightly quizzical expression will carry you through these long-winded proposals. Make sure to repeat these proposals only in encapsulated version, so as not to tire your celebrity unnecessarily.

All Armpieces and Trophies master the Laughing Head Toss. To practice, stand with feet in regulation "T" stance, left heel touching right instep. Arms are relaxed, one hand holds an aperitif. When given the signal, throw back head, toss blonde hair, and hunch shoulders slightly as if convulsed. Laugh encouragingly. Repeat. Never lose control and lapse into the vulgar Neophyte Horse Laugh, which can make the blonde look like she may be a bad security risk. The entire Laughing Head Toss cycle should be completed within 1.2 seconds. Use this laugh whenever candid party photographs are being taken. It will make your celebrity look like he's just said something marvelous.

o o o

One evening on a westbound flight to San Francisco, a few days after I had suddenly retired from being an Armpiece, I asked the handsome blond steward for a cup of tea. He brought me a Styrofoam cup half-filled with warm instant tea in tap water. I drank it without thinking.

When he came to pick up the cup, I was on autopilot. "Thank you!" I gushed, as if to Sirio Maccioni. "It was *really* delicious!" He looked down at me for a moment, and said, "Doesn't get much better than this, does it?" We both executed identical pro forma Laughing Head Tosses, looked at each other in a stunned moment of kindred ex-Armpiece recognition, then threw back our heads and just roared.

The Dark Side of Blonde

One morning when she was fifteen or so, my Russian grandmother heard a strange sound coming from the darkroom in their old gray house in Kazan.

We still have some pictures her father developed in that darkroom: a big, contrasty print of young cadets and side-saddled girls lined up on horseback, the field's grass black, a line of scrubby trees off to the right, no sky; a portrait of my nine-year-old grandmother in character as Neptune, with trident; a bizarre candid someone took of her haggard father and brother Dimitri on the morning after her mother died of scarlet fever.

But that particular morning she heard a scraping noise and looked toward the darkroom door just in time to see her younger brother Alik explode out of it.

She shrieked and put her hands to her face, thinking he had hidden on purpose to scare her. But he stood in the middle of the room dazed, blinking his eyes, dazzled by the morning sun, and a few moments passed before he noticed her there.

"Hullo, Lita," he said distractedly.

"Alik," she said, "why are you *doing that?*"

He paused and blinked at her for a moment, as if it was obvious why someone would shut himself up in a darkroom, wait in the dark until his eyes adjusted, then burst back out into the light.

"To see the contrast, Lita. The contrast!"

o o o

People want to step inside symbols that encompass opposites. Such images are deeply satisfying to us because they resolve duality. When you find an image that can mean two opposite things at the same time, you have stumbled upon a powerful symbol, a symbol that changes people's lives.

Man and woman, left and right, dark and light, good and evil, winter and spring—these are the fundamental opposites of human life. We have a foot in each camp. We are the fulcrum—the point at which non-meaning turns to meaning, where nonsense becomes sense for a while, then turns to nonsense again. We are strung up here between the unknowns of birth and death. But we are sensate and rational—we crave conclusion. Symbols that combine opposites give us one less shoelace to tie. They are complete within themselves, they give us a hope of completion, a hope of the final unity of opposites.

Blonde can mean innocence. It can mean that the woman wearing it is a muse, a spiritual guide. It can mean sun—warm sun or cool sun; it can mean perfection and it can mean the driving imperfection that is the ragged life force.

But the image also plays opposite itself, and blonde can mean death as well as life, chaos as well as order. Just as a picture of a footprint in the sand can look concave and then, by some odd mental switch, suddenly convex, so does the blonde go from sun to moon, from innocence to experience and back again.

○ ○ ○

Let's look at the duality of dark and light here for a moment, for blonde means both.

The Hebrew Bible hatchets the light from the dark starting with the very first words of Genesis:

> In the beginning God created the heaven and the earth.
> And the earth was without form, and void;
> And darkness was upon the face of the deep.
> And the spirit of God moved upon the face of the waters.
> And God said, Let there be light: and there was light.
> And God saw the light, that it was good:
> And God divided the light from the darkness.

This is where everything metaphorical starts in the Western canon. It is the beginning of difference—the beginning of "this is not that." Dark is unknown, light is known. Out of the chaos of darkness comes the light of understanding. The division of light and dark is the beginning of that which we recognize versus that which we choose to ignore.

As Westerners, we see dark and light as hopelessly divided. We spend much of life trying to get chaos under control. Let's get a fluorescent bulb out into that dark garage. Let's get those gold Combats—the big ones, for waterbugs. Let's sweep away dirt and darkness, and hope that dying never comes.

Iranian creation myths are also dualistic, and in them the "hot and moist, sweet-smelling, and light" is separated from the "cold and dry, heavy, dark, and stinking" by a huge void.

There's a giant, "Ymir" in Old Norse, who finds his counterparts in Iran and in India. He was one of those conveniently bisexual gods, the father and the mother to the giants. He appears in Iranian myth as Zurvan, and conceived twins, one "light and fragrant," the other "dark and stinking." The fair one created heaven and earth and everything that is beautiful or good. The dark one created "all the demons and everything evil."

It makes primal sense for humans to fear the dark and champion the light. Chaos and destruction wait right outside the ring of firelight—early man heard unidentified bone crunching out in the darkness and knew that there but for the grace of God crunched he. The mind registers its own limits on the continuum of time and matter. And this recognition leads us to prefer living to dying, order to chaos, and light to darkness.

If we can think, we are capable of rationality, of choice. This capability gives us the illusion of control over our lives and, in the end, the illusion of control over death. We value lucidity over confusion, for, as humans, confusion means losing the ordering principle by which we function and live. It means a scrapping of meaning.

Plato used the metaphors of light and dark to make his point about truth and goodness. He thought that the greatest thing a thinking person could do was to leave the cave of shadows and walk into the archetypal light, the "light" of the true source of being.

He used the image of the sun to represent "good," and said, in the *Republic,* that the sun acts on the visible world in the same way in which "good" affects the intellect. Plato thought that a philosopher's goal was to find the "luminous" knowledge that brings harmony between the human soul and the cosmic order of archetypes.

As Westerners, we've put a lot of time, money, and denial into trying to rid the world of death and darkness. Dark and light war with each other every night on TV. We glorify the light and repress the dark. And that's why we love sun blondes. By putting sun blonde in her hair, a woman aligns herself with that light. She plants her feet surely on the side of understanding, of consciousness. She follows along behind Plato like a duckling behind a mallard.

We are all involved in the game of dark and light. Which doors to consciousness we choose to open or to close depend just as much upon our ability to stand alone in a darkroom as upon our desire for bedazzlement.

Alik was dead, killed in the revolution, by the age of nineteen. When I was growing up, the fact of his early death made his boyhood talent seem all the more quirky and brilliant. Perhaps what it is to be human exists at the meeting of light and dark. Perhaps it's in the contrast.

o o o

Creation myths either divide light and dark or they mash them together. In our culture, we parse our blonde: We divide her into sun, moon, and innocent. But these are just her aspects. Taken together, all her parts fused, our blonde image symbolizes the wholeness of the mystical feminine.

Fusion is not new. The Old Norse took the fusion route, and their world rose from the combining of polarities: heat and cold, light and dark. Their creation myth, "The Prophesy of the Seeress," tells how the sons of Bur lifted the world from the sea, and fashioned Midgard—the world that mankind inhabits. When the sun shone from the south, the earth grew warm and was overgrown with green vegetation. The sun, moon, and stars were set on their courses, day and night established, and man and woman created:

> From the south the sun   by the side of the moon,
> heaved his right hand   over heaven's rim;
> the sun knew not   what seat he had
> the stars knew not   what stead they had
> the moon knew not   what might she had

The sun scrambled to its ordering place, but it had no idea where it was or what it could do. Our blondes are beacons of consciousness, but they do not know their own power, they don't know that they symbolize anything at all.

Eastern philosophies find the unity in dark and light, in yin and yang. Balance is the object, imbalance the cause of suffering. In order to appreciate the light, perhaps it is necessary to have been shut up in the darkroom. And in order to tolerate the darkroom, maybe we need to know that the light is out there.

When George Gordon, Lord Byron wrote

> She walks in beauty, like the night
> Of cloudless climes and starry skies;
> And all that's best of dark and bright
> Meet in her aspect and her eyes:
> Thus mellowed to the tender light
> Which heaven to gaudy day denies. . . .

he was not talking about a blonde. He was talking about the idea that beauty comes from the balance of opposites—from the balance of light and dark. He was describing the calm beauty of the balanced psyche. Let's face it. He was talking about a brunette.

o o o

It makes primal sense for humans to fear the dark and crave the light, but what does it do to culture? What happens when we start dividing out dark from light, using people as living metaphors?

My friend Andrea gave me a call early one evening and said, "Come on over here, I want to show you something," so I went across the street to her apartment. She was looking at some footage she had shot for *Promised Land,* a film she produced for the National Museum of American Jewish History. She does that kind of thing. Anyway, I went over.

The tape was an interview of a Jewish woman who had been hidden from the Nazis by a non-Jewish German family. She and her mother are the only members of her family who survived the Holocaust.

When Andrea interviewed her, the woman was in her late fifties. They discussed her family, her experiences, and then there was a long silence on the tape. The woman looked down. Then she said, "I went to a Jewish kindergarten. Every day, more children disappeared. I had the good fortune of blonde [hair] and blue eyes. That's why I keep my hair light. It's sort of a little safety thing. I always have to feel safe."

o o o

Carl Jung believed that every person has a "Shadow," a repressed "dark side" of the psyche that draws its strength from the primal psychic urges that society refuses to find appropriate. All that smashing down of inappropriate urges makes for a big, concealed power inside you. Refusing to acknowledge that power, that Shadow within ourselves, leads us to project it onto other people.

That's how you find yourself suddenly hating someone for no obvious reason. That person has something about him that is exactly like what you repress within yourself. The more you suppress the Shadow, the more you project it onto other people.

Whole societies project away as blithely as individuals do.

The more unbalanced a society, the more repressed its Shadow, and the greater its expression of hatred toward the "dark" side. Victorian England repressed all mention of sexuality, yet pornography has never seen such a flowering. The psyche, individual or public, is like a balloon. Squeeze it in one place and it will bulge in another.

o o o

Insanity lives in the idea of blonde. The Holocaust was a huge example of projection—of the repression of the cultural Shadow side. If you are going along thinking how pure and golden you are, what do you do with your repressed dark side? You project it onto a scapegoat.

The Holocaust happened under the banner of the blond warrior-hero. Although blond hair was only a minor part of the patched-together Aryan "myth," it gave a quick and easily understood image to the Nazi fantasia.

The fact that Aryan blond is a male blond image should clue us in to something. You don't see a lot of women on those posters of Hitler youth. You see boys looking upward toward the sunny future. And boys remind us of Apollo. After all the talk of Tibet, and Atlantis, and the Nibelungenlied, and going back to primitive strengths, and so on, it's really Apollo the Nazis co-opted.

In the Nazi plan, woman was in service to the blond god, the SS trooper, the homoerotic sun god. She was babymaker and instigator of male "heroism." Young blonde women from the "right families" were urged to have as many babies as they could, fathered by members of the SS. A woman's individuality had no value.

Along with determining to rid itself of all people who were not of "Aryan blood," the cult of the Apollonian in Nazi Germany—a cult that had its roots in the previous century—was a put-down of all that is goddess rather than god. It was a put-down of all that is creative rather than intellectual, warm rather than cool, terrestrial rather than sky cult.

At its most destructive, blond champions duality, not balance, not fusion. Our blonde echoes the racist myth-making of Friedrich Nietzsche's *Genealogy of Morals,* published in 1887:

> At the core of all these aristocratic races the beast of prey is not to be mistaken, the magnificent blond beast, avidly rampant for spoil and victory.

In our generation, the idea of blonde echoes that male Aryan ideal. This is the truth about blondes that we all agree never to mention, the dark side of blonde that we all repress. Blonde is a racial statement. "I am of the light people," it says, "not of the dark people." "I am aligned with the mythically male, not the female. Don't hurt me." In America, as in all Western countries, it really *is* safer to be blonde.

In his novel *Diana: The Goddess Who Hunts Alone,* Carlos Fuentes's main character, a middle-aged Mexican novelist, arrives at the house of his estranged lover:

> . . . I found Diana, divided by the light of the gallery at nightfall, half light, half shadow, perfectly cut in two,

like one of Ingres' female portraits. . . . She walked toward me, separated from herself by the light, yielding not an inch of her luminous person to her dark person, or vice versa. The contrast was such that even her short blonde hair seemed white on the side of the gallery window and black on the wall side.

When the two halves of blonde don't talk to each other—when the light is hatcheted from the dark—in the way in which Fuentes's Diana is cut in two by the light of the gallery at nightfall, the image does not do its mythic job of resolving discrepancy, and we wander, lost in the dark wood of the unconscious.

One afternoon in 1987, a twenty-nine-year-old chemistry student named Jonathan Haynes walked into a San Francisco hair salon and shot one of the stylists to death. He recognized his victim, Frank Ringi, from an early morning TV show. Six years later, Haynes made an appointment with a Chicago-area plastic surgeon named Martin Sullivan, walked into his office, and shot and killed him too.

Immediately after his arrest in 1993, Haynes confessed to both crimes. "I despise fake Aryan cosmetics and I wanted to give voice to my disgust by killing Frank Ringi," Haynes said. "He makes his living as a hair colorist. . . . It's the business of changing hair from brunette to blonde that got him killed." Haynes said that he wanted to stop the proliferation of "fake Aryan beauty"; Sullivan had sculpted "Aryan noses," Ringi had dyed his clients' hair blonde.

o o o

I keep remembering the *New Yorker* cartoon from the forties that pictured two men standing in the snow on a sidewalk. The big guy has obviously just shoveled down through the cement to the sewer line and the dirt below. The other man is saying something like, "No, no, Harry—just the white fluffy stuff on top!"

This should be a white fluffy stuff kind of book, but every once in a while, when shoveling down through blondes, you hit a sewer line.

Moon Blonde

No one read us those traditional limb-whacking, frog-talking fairy tales when we were young. My Southern grandmother thought they were too brutal, and I think they revolted my mother. The hacking off of heads, the sprouting of new heads, the shutting up of Rapunzel in the tower, the grinding of Cinderella into the ashes—these didn't seem to be the kind of thing a child should hear while drifting off to sleep. Consequently, we stuck with Pooh.

Bruno Bettelheim argued that children need fairy tales because they give an outlet to the morbid fantasies that all children have. Though heads are chopped off, they sprout again. Though Rapunzel is locked in the tower, she circumvents the lock. Though Cinderella is ground into servitude by her half-sisters, she rides off with the prince in the end, leaving them to grouse among themselves. How satisfying.

Though no one at home read those tales to my sisters and me, somehow we learned all of them. They were ubiquitous—heard in school, spoofed in cartoons, watered down in the big, oversize children's books of childhood friends. Had we missed them, perhaps none of us would be a blonde today, for fairy tales are one of the greatest of our society's hair-color inculcation devices.

Most of the heroines of those fairy tales are blonde—Goldilocks, Cinderella, Little Red Riding Hood, Sleeping Beauty (also known as Briar Rose), Rapunzel. As Marina Warner tells us in her book *From the Beast to the Blonde,* in fairy tales, blonde hair is a metaphor for virtue, a metaphor for value, desirability, fecundity, and purity.

Though I did not hear much at home about Hansel and Gretel or Beauty and the Beast—a tale we now picture on Disney's terms—my grandmother read us *Winnie-the-Pooh, The Wind in the Willows,* and a Finnish book about a velvety white hippolike creature called Moomintroll.

My mother loved *Moomintroll.* Its characters wandered about at midnight on Midsummer Eve, picking flowers and wearing them in circlets round their ears. They had adventures—were washed away by floods and took up residence in floating theaters. And I remember Moominmamma's making a tiny dinghy out of bark, which she launched quietly in a brackish pool as the first ashes of an erupting volcano floated down upon her head.

My mother also had a soft spot for fairies. She loved *The Blue Fairy Book,* the sprites of *Down Spiderweb Lane* (a book about a child's adventures in an overgrown bit of her own back garden). These were the fairies of the children's books that had been hers when she was a child, and she and my grandmother read them to us. She loved the little creatures of Victorian faerie, the ones that danced in glimmering rings in the darkening violet of evening woods.

Those fairies came down to us from the nurses of the Victorian English. Wealthier families employed women to look after their children. These nurses repeated the rustic and traditional stories that had been forgotten by their employers.

Faerie is its own world, a whole world, a whole separate stratum of consciousness. Unlike the Grimm tales, these fairy stories were more about existing than about doing. They were not so much about the character and what happened to him— turned into a toad, kissed a prince, whacked a head—but about how mankind, nature, and the mystical rub up against each other. Faerie's inhabitants lived on the breath of the night wind, like the small gnats of Keats's river sallows.

Down Spiderweb Lane opened a door to another entire world for me, and when, as a child, I entered that world, I stood outside my own reality. As Tolkien would say, I learned to hold communion with other living things, and surveyed the depths of space and time.

By the time the fairies got to us, through the drawings and the pastel-washed etchings, they were graceful, shimmering beings with translucent wings and disheveled blonde hair.

They were Innocent Blondes, but they had a not-so-innocent leader—Queen Maeve, the Queen of Faerie.

In my mother's old fairy-tale books, Maeve had been reformed into a guardian and protectress of fairy borders. She had been cleaned up a bit, for she didn't start out that way. That queen had another blonde in her character. She was my first Moon Blonde.

Marie Bonaparte has written:

> This story ... bears witness to my desire to escape from my familiar surroundings and become an omnipotent woman, or fairy, in a supernaturally free domain.

And the story of blonde bears witness to the same urge in women—it is the story of longing: to survey the depths of space and time? Perhaps, if you think about surveying as a going out toward the unknown. To escape gray hair and laundry? Yes. But especially to become an omnipotent woman in a supernaturally free domain.

Summer Wheat Blondes, Innocent Blondes, Apollo Blondes—none of these is in charge of her own life. Summer Wheat's fortunes are bound to home and family. The Innocent has a protector. Apollo Blondes lean heavily on the constructs of society. The only omnipotent blonde we've ever had was the old Moon Goddess, the original Moon Blonde.

o o o

Rosemary Guiley tells us that the goddess—the triple goddess—"she of a thousand names," is worshiped and petitioned in many guises. Her three aspects mimic the life cycle of woman: She is the virgin, the mother, and the crone. Her faces are related to the phases of the moon, for the moon is so bound up in woman's physiognomy. The new moon is Artemis or Diana, the virgin goddess, wild, free, and unencumbered. The waning moon is the crone, the old woman past menopause. She's represented as a hag, the destroyer to whom all living things return at the end. And the full moon is the mother, the matron and the nurturer. She is Selene, Demeter, Ishtar, Isis, and in Irish folklore, Queen Maeve.

This is a very common view of the mythical female; it is the woman-as-moon-goddess approach. Notice that there is no sun in here, no earth. People who go for this story think of woman as related to night, darkness, and the reflected light of the sun.

Queen Maeve, or Mab—hearty, maternal, in control—ran her faerie kingdom with zest and vigor. But we've taken the zest and vigor out of our Moon Blonde. On the drugstore shelf she's only a shade of her former self. A very light shade. Summer Wheat Blonde has taken over her maternity department. Apollo Blonde is running all her organizations. Innocent Blonde took over her virginal aspects. Since we don't like crones and hags, she's lost a lot of shelf space. She gets the role of erotic destroyer. It's really the only slot left.

o o o

If the woman you are looking at has hair the color of platinum—if she is narrow, languid, nocturnal, sleeps late, prefers to be photographed in black and white, and likes cats—she's our current Moon Blonde.

She has very narrow hips, a primal signal that she is not interested in having children. (Sometimes Moon Blondes steal children, through spell, witchcraft, or divorce settlement, but they rarely bear them.) She tends to wear satin, a fabric at once slinky and reflective.

You'll see her in the movies, where the highly constructed conditions of makeup and good lighting combine satisfactorily with Champagne in her trailer, people to support her, and a hairdresser trailing behind.

But you'll also see Moon Blondes in trailer parks, where they have time on their hands and no hope of salvation. There they turn their minds to destruction: There's no other way out.

Our Moon Blonde is decadent. She is a projection of the female Shadow. She gives us an outlet for morbid fantasies. Everything about the mythical feminine that our society chooses not to recognize—every vicious, mean, aggressive, brutal, unforgiving thing about the dark side of woman—is expressed in our Moon Blonde. She is Marlene Dietrich in *The Blue Angel*. She is very powerful, but she is always vanquished in movies and on TV. We can't let her get out of control. Sooner or later she always pays the price for all her sociopathic behavior.

Sun Blondes symbolize the life force. One way or another, they foster creation. Innocent Blondes inspire us to spiritual heights. Summer Wheat Blondes have children and make homes. Apollo Blondes master hierarchies, burn to get to the top. But the Moon Blonde is a destroyer. She symbolizes perverse desire, she symbolizes the death wish. But, oh—she's so attractive.

She's the goddess of moon and starlight, of evening, the underworld, death and chaos. Her predecessor Hecate ruled over death, despair, and destruction, as well as over seasonal changes, womanhood, and life cycles; her ancestor Selene was goddess of the moon; Persephone, goddess of sleep. Later on, Venus, absorbing some of Hecate's traits, was not just a sex kitten, but could destroy a man's will, his life power, his integrity. Our current Moon Blonde carries these traits genetically.

Falling for a Moon Blonde is like flinging yourself out a window. On the way down, you realize that giving in to the atavistic desire to fly may not have been such a good idea after all. But it's too late. She is the female vertigo, and is likely to bring on a confused, disoriented state of mind. Glenn Close plays a terrific Moon Blonde in *Fatal Attraction*. Faye Dunaway plays a really scary one in *The Three Musketeers*. They both come to bad ends. Much knifing and chopping.

Summer Wheat Blondes are sexy, but Moon Blondes are erotic. There's a big difference between sexiness and eroticism. Sexuality is the urge to procreation, whereas eroticism is the art of creating desire. Betty Grable was sexy—she inspired a whole generation of soldiers to keep fighting so that they could come back to that nice woman and have a passel of kids. Marlene Dietrich was erotic—she was not about keeping the home fires burning. Not that kind of home fire.

Moon Blondes fire unquenchable longing. They are interested in conquering, but have no desire to colonize. They destroy things—lives, marriages, cars. They tend to throw china—you'll lose your Viennese dessert plates. They love chaos, are out for themselves, are illicit, claw bearing, scrappy, bitchy, and lethal. Like Glenn Close, Moon Blonde again in *Dangerous Liaisons*.

You'll often hear Moon Blondes described with the metaphors of war: She's a bombshell, a knockout, dynamite, striking. She is a threat to stability, she is a crisis.

o o o

In the drugstore, Moon Blonde is the lightest of the ash blonde shades: The lighter the ash, the more lethal the blonde. Ash Blondes, like the Winter Wheat Blonde, still make an effort toward civility, toward family. But they tend to blue and violet, to tones of coolness; in the final analysis, to tones of death. They are "ash" as in "Ashes, ashes, we all fall down."

Since most Dark Ash Blondes fall into the "cover the gray" category, and are not so much impersonating blondeness as matching their own hair color, we won't spend much time on them. The interesting blonde is blonde "on purpose"; she picks a shade out of the barrel and chooses to wear it on her head.

All those Champagne, Starlight, and Mist blondes fall in right behind our Moon Blonde. They are her coterie. You have to make a serious effort to be blonde like that, you have to strip your hair and put the starlight or the Champagne back into it.

And so these lighter ash blondes are symbolic—they do mean something. They are the blondes of evening, of alcohol and forgetting. Think of Grace Kelly playing opposite Cary Grant, all evening dresses, diamonds, and starlight.

The French have made this kind of blonde a specialty. Think of the great Catherine Deneuve, aloof perfection, or Jacqueline François, a singer who covered Edith Piaf's songs in the fifties with a voice like warm Armagnac. Perhaps the French had this blonde in mind when they thought up the rowdy song lyrics, "Auprès de ma blonde, il fait bon, fait bon!"

o o o

In his huge book *The White Goddess: A Historical Grammar of Poetic Myth,* Robert Graves was one of the first to try to prove that there once was a primeval matriarchy and a great goddess. (He tried to hammer a bit too much into unity with that one, but it was a noble effort.)

Even though he was enamored of the goddess, he thought a woman could only be a muse and never a poet—that she could never be a creator. He thought the goddess's great role was to inspire heterosexual poems as answer to the longing she created. He thought that she prevented the spread of "sentimental homosexuality." And the way she did that was by focusing man's poetic attention on her. She could not create, she could only be an inspiration. She could reflect, never generate, like the moon. This is the flaw in his book. But I digress.

Graves had a huge impact with his goddess, and she is a Moon Blonde. He describes her as a lovely, pale and slender woman with "lips red as rowan-berries, startlingly blue eyes, and long fair hair." She is a shape-shifter, and can suddenly transform herself into a sow, a mare, a bitch, a vixen, a she-ass, a weasel, a serpent, an owl, a she-wolf, a tigress, a mermaid, or a loathsome hag. What a handful. No time for paying the mortgage with this gal. She is exhausting, yet a man wants her more as his strength flags. Graves has described a vampire.

Coleridge describes a Moon Blonde in the "Rime of the Ancient Mariner":

> *Her* lips were red, *her* looks were free,
> Her locks were yellow as gold:
> Her skin was as white as leprosy,
> The Nightmare Life-in-Death was she,
> Who thicks man's blood with cold.

She is the "Nightmare Life-in-Death." And here we are, back again to light and dark, spring and winter. This blonde plays dark to the sun blonde's light, but is a duality within herself as well: She is a living death.

o o o

Just a side note about yellow. Coleridge says her "locks were yellow as gold," and something about that image doesn't ring healthy. Sounds jaundiced, urinal. It is unusual for blondes to be described positively as having yellow hair. Ruth Mellinkoff tells us that, in classical Athens, prostitutes customarily dyed their hair yellow. In Rome, too, prostitutes wore blonde wigs. Sermons at the end of the thirteenth century regularly re-minded parishioners that none were to wear yellow headbands or veils except Jewesses, prostitutes, and concubines. In *The Merry Wives of Windsor,* Shakespeare uses yellow to invoke the brother-killing Cain: "He hath but a little wee face, with a little yellow beard—a Cain-coloured beard."

Geler is the Yiddish word for "yellow-haired," and it has a negative connotation, evidently stemming from the legend that Moses burned the golden calf, ground it to a powder, mixed it with water, and had the Israelites drink it. The people who had prostrated themselves to the idol were immediately struck with injuries.

Yellow is generally a pejorative designation. Even Yeats's poem "For Anne Gregory" leaves us with a faint feeling that she has somehow been maligned with a compliment:

> 'Never shall a young man,
> Thrown into despair
> By those great honey-coloured
> Ramparts at your ear,
> Love you for yourself alone
> And not your yellow hair.'

> 'But I can get a hair-dye
> And set such colour there,
> Brown, or black, or carrot,
> That young men in despair
> May love me for myself alone
> And not my yellow hair.'

> 'I heard an old religious man

But yesternight declare
That he had found a text to prove
That only God, my dear,
Could love you for yourself alone
And not your yellow hair.'

o o o

You don't see too many Moon Blondes on the street—she's not up when you are. And she's not exactly a people person. She wants to be alone, hides from the light, turns her face from the public. Moonlight becomes her. It goes with her hair.

Greta Garbo disappeared into Moon Blondeness—she was a smiling teenager, but learned her role so well that she ended as a recluse. The singer Blondie did a good Moon Blonde imitation twenty years ago, but actually was just a nice suburban girl apt to cook fish for you at the apartment if you looked hungry. This time around, she looks more Moon—but I bet she has *The New Basics Cookbook* on her shelf. Courtney Love was a great white-trash Moon Blonde co-dependent, but now has had all that tucked and lifted and is telling women's magazines her workout strategy.

The Moon Blonde is a projection of our fantasy of the dark side of the female, and we see her more frequently in advertising and movies than we do on the subway. When you do see a Moon Blonde on the street or at a gallery opening or taking your money at the bakery, it is time to look closely at her. She is screaming something to you.

I've had students who show up on the first day of my class as

Moon Blonde as Hecate, and with so many tattoos and piercings that they look as if they got in a fight with a carpet stapler. I take a look at the zombie blankness in the eyes and think to myself, "This kid is trouble." And then she opens her mouth and says something like, "Can I get you an herb tea from the cart?" You never can tell with blondes.

These Moon Blondes are young. They still have feeling left in their scalps. They are proclaiming their independence from home, from responsibility, from "the normal." It is interesting that there are certain appropriate ways to profess one's ignoring of socially accepted behavior. The imitation of sociopathology has its own strict dress code. Moon hair, yes. Lack of deodorant, no.

If you run across an old Moon Blonde, keep running. The old ones are the real ones. The real ones are the deadly ones—passive-aggressive, "weak" and vicious.

The Moon Blonde image is a relief for women—a relief from having to be the nice girl. Even if we never go platinum ourselves, we can secretly relish that other women do. The Moon Blonde says things we would never say, does things we would never do. She is outrageous, and we applaud.

Perhaps the most beautiful reference to a Moon Blonde is in the ballad "The Holy Land of Walsinghame," quoted by Graves:

> There is a maiden in the noble house
> Surpassing all women of Ireland.
> She steps forward, with yellow hair,
> Beautiful and many gifted.

Her discourse with each man in turn
Is beautiful, is marvellous,
The heart of each one breaks
With longing and love for her.

○ ○ ○

No discussion of Moon Blonde would be complete without talking about Madonna. People always say to me, "Oh, Moon Blonde—like Madonna?" And now we find ourselves on some very slippery turf.

Madonna is not truly a Moon Blonde, but she does a great imitation. She plays a terrific night crawler in *Dick Tracy*. And she's had her Moon Blonde moments—her *Sex* book, and farther back her whole lacy-undressed-and-crosses look was a good stab at Moon Blondeness.

But a Moon Blonde is a destroyer, not a creator. A true Moon Blonde could never run the business that Madonna runs. Madonna dances, sings, works out, had a baby. She was just trying to get out of Michigan. Moon Blondes don't work, they don't sweat, and they don't bear children. They expect people, money, and things to come to them.

Madonna's well-documented talent has always been her ability to identify the public's mythological need of the moment. She's a contemporary shape shifter—she can play Eva Perón, Marilyn, a matador's lover, a New Age innocent, and still get home in time for a healthy vegetarian dinner prepared by her personal chef.

Madonna's got more in common with Martha Stewart than

with Jean Harlow. She gives women what they want, she gives men what they want. She's a marketer, like Martha.

By being able to play so many characters, Madonna gives us the impression that she is resolving fundamental opposites—she plays dark and light, Moon Blonde and Innocent Blonde—and can mean more than one thing at a time. But she is never truly in the dark, never truly in the light. Her meaning is on the surface. She is like a highway billboard over which car headlights slide, and she means to be.

Madonna is never taken to mean anything serious, except by media studies Ph.D. candidates. She doesn't take herself seriously. No one's heart breaks with longing or with love for her. She's an Ironic Postmodern Reference to a Blonde—a Blonde with one raised eyebrow.

Ironic Blonde

My friend Thomas invited me to a silent auction recently, and I accepted, for he swims in an interesting pond.

We met in design school. He was in architecture, and spent a lot of time out on the lawn as professors urged him to explore "alternative quantitative systems" by measuring copiers with ears of corn. I was in graphic design, learning what things "wanted." As in, "That page wants to move over there," "That line of type wants to be bigger," and "That photo wants to come right off the edge." After a few semesters of this, I wanted to go right off the edge, and Tom threw down his corn at approximately the same moment.

Thomas is the kind of guy who runs off to help sketch out a

pool-house addition for Jasper Johns when he's not designing a twelve-foot mahogany dining table for his own loft. I do not do these things. I consider it a great day if I find tuna for sixty-nine cents a can. We have different yardsticks of happiness. Mine is round and holds albacore.

Gallery parties are not my usual venue. My usual venue is my one-room home. Nevertheless, when invited by Thomas, I go. On the appointed evening, I found him in a converted warehouse gallery by the Hudson, surrounded by friends and admirers. He welcomed me charmingly. We sipped white wine from cool glasses and thought about how wonderful we were to be sipping white wine from cool glasses.

All was a whirl of white walls and young women wearing reembroidered acid-green chiffon dresses. Lots of serious fashion moved about. Angular male models wore flat khaki jackets and flat khaki pants. Everyone was incredibly beautiful, and young, and clipped and pale and expensive.

I wore my usual large, body-hiding knit pieces—a long black dress to the ground and a large oatmeal-colored overtop. My hair was huge, unkempt and Summer Wheat. This was totally wrong for the evening, totally out of sync, yet the sort of ensemble in which one doesn't hesitate to ease out one's stomach during a conversation about the merit of a Robert Longo.

I was particularly pleased with my choice of shoes: big, flat, fisherman's sandals. They certainly were a contrast to the strappy pastel spikes about me. As it turns out, I looked a bit like Moses. More than one person mentioned the resemblance. I just needed tablets.

Everyone was a painter or had a book out or had shot a photograph that was being auctioned. The hors d'oeuvres leaned toward the Asian. A crumpled grape tart lay casually in a basket. Artisanal breads were tossed about in heaps. A large earthenware bowl of bruised-looking olives stood under a Motherwell sketch.

It was the kind of gallery experience where you think you probably have more in common with the caterers than with the guests until you get to the head of the drinks line and find that they, too, are hipper than you.

I wandered about, surrounded by photographers and ex-dancers, knowing no one but Thomas and trying not to interfere with his labyrinthian social construct—everyone he knew seemed to have converged on this particular event. Thomas alternately dodged, ducked, turned pleasedly, stepped in, stepped out, and smiled across a crowded room. This seamless activity had the look of social tai chi.

Crowds depress me. They always make me think of the carnivals they put up in mall parking lots, *Ship of Fools* and all that. I tried to get my mind off the turgid ebb and flow of human misery by convincing a woman to bid on Yul Brynner's original *King and I* jacket. It was an amazing, ethereal, silk translucence of magenta warp and gold weft, pinned like a rare butterfly to the wall. After I muscled her into buying it, I found myself falling for his *King and I* John Lobb velvet slippers, which sported a hand-embroidered *YB*. I surreptitiously placed my fisherman foot on the floor next to the slipper podium. I eyeballed. Oh, for an ear of corn. These shoes wanted to be on my feet.

I pictured myself strolling about my one-room home eating

tuna on a muffin while wearing a fluffy robe and Yul's large black John Lobbs.

After this vision I felt unaccountably morose, and began circling again, a whale shark in knitwear. It was then that I felt the strange messianic twinge.

The last time I felt a twinge like that I found myself witnessing about the dual nature of the godhead to a food photographer on a kitchen set. The doctor says I have to be careful. So I went and got another white wine, and found Thomas and said, "I am Lazarus, come from the dead." But he just smiled and introduced me to Gloria Steinem.

Now, were I twenty, I would have pretended that I didn't recognize her. But my age of irony has passed. No longer do I mock feeling, genuine or induced. No longer do I hide the Current holiday wrap catalog when friends drop in. Nor am I ashamed to say that I always get a warm feeling from the Christmas card that shows two scarved mice hugging each other in glee while shooting downhill on a bobsled. I have heard the rodents singing, each to each.

So I told her how much I admired her, and she was gracious and charming and, as you'd expect, wise and funny, and after a while I offered her a way out of talking with me, for I remember well the celebrity-hammerlock problem at events. A famous feminist friend of hers was stuck in the lambent armpiece role, just because her face wasn't as well-known, and we chatted for a while. I was about to wander off, happy, when I remembered the blonde book.

So I told Gloria Steinem all about her seventies blondeness—about how she had used those jumbo highlights in the

front of her hair to make herself seem accessible, unthreaten-
ing, childlike—an Innocent. How her blondeness had made
her difficult message palatable to middle America, how she
had become the poster blonde of the women's movement. I was
really pleased with my astute observations.

"No," she said.

I really hated hearing that "No." But I smiled.

"No," she said, "I was making a statement. In those days,
women didn't advertise that they colored their hair. I put those
streaks in to be radical. I was imitating Holly Golightly."

In other words, she was an Ironic Blonde.

o o o

The first thing they teach you in semiotics boot camp is that
whatever message you think you are sending out—loud and as
clear as a bell—is not what your audience is hearing. You say,
"Hot enough for you?," with your usual aplomb, and the guy
at the water fountain thinks you've said, "I see by your perspiration that you could lose twenty pounds."

Irony is the use of words or images to convey the opposite of
their literal meaning. It depends on contrast—a contrast
between apparent and intended meaning. The problem at the
water fountain occurs when the apparent meaning is not
apparent and the intended meaning is not intended.

Now the problem with trying to flip-flop the meaning
of blonde occurs because the symbol means so many things.
It means many things as a cultural symbol, and then you have
all those personal associations slathered on top. The mask

of blonde is not always consciously assumed.

Trying to be Ironic Blonde is hard because the apparent meaning of blonde is so fragmented. It's like trying to roll an overstuffed omelet out of a sticky pan. Some images just won't flip.

Mae West achieved Ironic Blonde because she flipped a particular kind of blonde: She made Moon Blonde funny. She undercut her elaborately coiffed and boned eroticism with a killing sense of humor. She follows up her best-known line "Come up and see me, sometime" (in the movie *My Little Chickadee*) with the less well-known "Come Wednesday night, that's amateur night."

Jenny McCarthy, a former Playmate of the Year, satirized her Vanna White–like Young Summer Wheat role even as she performed it on *Singled Out!,* an MTV dating game. Rebecca Romijn, a *Sports Illustrated* swimsuit model, spoofed her own California Blonde–highlighted image when she appeared in a yellow bikini, French maid's apron, and high heels to feather-dust rocks and trees on a Miller Lite desert island; Candice Bergen parodied Apollo Blonde in *Murphy Brown*.

Which poses the great blonde question: If a blonde in a bikini and a French maid's apron winks at the camera to advise us that she is just *imitating* a blonde in a bikini and a French maid's apron, does the guy opening a beer at the refrigerator see her as a savvy satirist of contemporary popular culture? Or does he just see a blonde in a bikini? And what does the seven-year-old girl on the sofa see? There's a certain *Bridge on the River Kwai* dilemma in Ironic Blondeness.

When you first saw her face on a book jacket, did you read

Gloria Steinem's blonde hair as a one-eyebrow-raised-ironic-reference-to-the-American-beauty-machine-intended-to-keep-woman-unhappy-unfulfilled-and-forever-buying-more? Or did you think, "Hey, what a sweet-looking gal. I can't believe she's a feminist."

Steinem may have thought she was poking fun at blondeness when she put in those streaks, but the contrast she set off in the mind of middle America was between her innocent looks and her feminist brain. Her accessible blondeness opened their ears to her. And that, to my mind, is ironic.

o o o

Last night I lay inert upon my bed, thinking of certain subtle refinements I planned to make to my signature dish, basil chicken roll-ups. I was just sprinkling my mental chicken breasts with Parmigiano-Reggiano when an E! program about the history of the *Playboy* centerfold came on.

By the time I focused on the TV, Pamela Anderson Lee was saying glowing things about how *Playboy* started her career, and about how her *Baywatch* stint grew out of her posing as a centerfold. I went on mentally sprinkling cheese.

But when Pamela—a California Blonde—began talking about the many people who write to ask about her surgeries, my mental roll-ups vanished and I turned up the sound.

"What have you had done," fans ask, "to your face, to your breasts, to your fat in order to be so completely perfect?" Pamela told us candidly that she had endured only one surgery—breast enhancement.

She was measuring up very nicely with her blonded hair and her nice body, but when she "enhanced" her breasts, she crossed over to perfection. Apollo's fingerprints are all over *Baywatch*.

We've come a long way from 1956, the year Shirley Polykoff wrote "Does she . . . or doesn't she?," the first big hair-color ad campaign. Hair coloring was a relatively small industry before that time, with annual sales of 25 million. But by 1966, sales were at 200 million, and nearly half of all American women regularly colored their hair. Polykoff kept sales pumping with copy lines like "Is it true that blondes have more fun?" and "If I've only one life to live, let me live it as a blonde."

But then it was all a secret. If you colored your hair, you didn't mention it. That's where Polykoff's original idea for the famous Clairol tag line came from: Her future mother-in-law asked her son, in Yiddish, "Well, does she, or doesn't she?" after their first meeting.

I knew that we'd come out of the closet since Shirley's time. I knew that most women do something to their hair, and that they're very open about it. But I also knew that they feel much worse about their looks than they did forty years ago, that the dream of physical perfection torments the mature sun-wheat-and-growth blonde as she has that piece of Sacher torte.

I knew that Apollo reminded our fertility blonde to have the small dinner salad, for no one likes a cheerleader who chunks up. But I really hadn't realized that he had gotten such a hold on us until I heard Pamela and thought about how surgery is just part of the package now. Face-lifts, liposuction, Botox, foil, highlighting caps, and double-processing: The veil has been lifted in the last forty years. The value of "natural beauty" has given way to the battering ram of enhancement processes. We accept alteration as appropriate, as perfunctory, as normal. And when we hear that Pamela's decided to de-hance her breasts, well, we accept that, too.

o o o

Today I went to have a mammogram. I get afraid, so I usually hide my fears by yelling at the staff. But this time I vowed not to yell at the staff, and took a book with me in order to bring along some comfort from the continuity of my real life. I wanted to avoid the banality of doctor's office magazines—magazines like *American Duckhunter,* which I probably wouldn't choose to read if I were not dressed in a blue paper robe and sitting in a hallway. I grabbed from the top of my research pile and stuck a book in my bag on the way out the door.

"Is this your first time here?"

"No."

"Fill this out."

The charm, the caring, the healer instinct. I marveled at their lack.

> Last name: Ilyin
>
> First name: Natalia
>
> Nature of visit: follow-up mammogram
>
> Any history of breast cancer in your family? Yes
>
> If so, relationship: Mother

I dutifully filled out the form, wondering why they always

had me fill out a "first visit" form, even after so many visits.

The waiting room was crowded. Three new people came in: a placid, fifties-ish woman in sweats; a soft, polite older man; and a woman in her mid-seventies with the giveaway hair, a mussed salt-and-pepper crew cut. We smiled at each other. Her smile was bright, her eyes large, in the vinyl waiting room with its lamps on in the middle of the day, and its clipboards, and its stand-up cards about AIDS walks propped on French provincial side tables.

I pulled the book out of my bag. I expected Nor Hall's *The Moon and the Virgin.* But the book I pulled out was *Dolly: My Life and Other Unfinished Business,* by Dolly Parton. Of such is synchronicity.

o o o

Now there are people I know I should admire, like Gandhi. And then there are people I really do admire, like Dolly Parton. Here is a woman known for the size of her breasts. Now try that on for a moment. Every time you go downstairs for a bagel, people are talking about your breasts. She is saddled with a cartoon of a female body—the world's first female female impersonator. Someone once asked Dolly how long it took to do her huge blonde hair. "I don't know," said she, "I'm never there." She's smart, she's funny, she's got guts. She is the quintessential jackass rig.

In sailing terminology, a jackass rig is any combination of square rig and fore-and-aft rig on a sailing ship having two or more masts. It's also known as a hermaphrodite rig, and it is a strange-looking thing when you see it sailing up the river. Dolly is rigged like that—most blondes are rigged like that. Most blondes are two kinds of blonde at once. Take Goldie Hawn: she's an Apollo crossed with an Innocent. Or Anne Heche, Innocent and Moon; or Camilla Parker Bowles, Moon and Summer Wheat; or Tina Turner: those highlights are Summer Wheat at home, Moon Blonde on stage. Most of us are combo plates, Mutt Blonde. But Dolly is the sublime example of an Apollonian/Summer Wheat cross:

> Many an old boy has found out too late that I look like a woman but I think like a man. It is a great mistake to assume that because I look soft, I do business that way. Just like the first prostitute who realized that she was "sittin' on a gold mine," I know what I have to sell, and nobody goes prospecting in my gold mine without first buying the mineral rights.

She's selling those breasts, that childlike singing voice, that vision of the old Tennessee home place. Dolly's Summer Wheat side had the urge to nurture the people in the depressed county where she grew up. Her Apollonian side created a structure for that urge: Dollywood. But that Apollonian side also urges her to overhaul herself with plastic surgery, and tries to subdue her Summer Wheat body.

She makes music and does business from her male sun side, but the inspiration for her songs comes from her female sun side—she sings about birth, death, and regeneration.

The blonde, our blonde, is caught between being an Apol-

Ionian and an earth goddess. She uses language, mathematics, poetry, music. But her head is divided from her body, a body that cycles through menstruation once a month. She is schooled in the rationality and measuring of her culture, but her body bears witness to her grounding in nature.

Right now, I'm thinking about RuPaul. Now here's a guy who has straddled a duality or two in his time. He is a leonine Summer Wheat Blonde, Apollonian bodied (but of course). He has his gossipy show—gossip is watered-down Moon. But he poses as a human letter form, clad in red vinyl, for an AIDS research–benefiting ad. Now what could be more Apollo?

If you are interested in symbols that resolve discrepancy, look to RuPaul. Though he has a foot in every camp, the most interesting thing about RuPaul is his philosophy, a philosophy he airs on every broadcast.

Whatever you think yourself to be, he reminds us, be proud, be strong, and don't take any abuse. His philosophy reminds me of the moral of *Tootsie:* Sometimes it takes a gender switcher to instill confidence in those of us who are clothed in female bodies.

o o o

"Gentlemen always seem to remember blondes," said Anita Loos, and the one they seem to remember most is still Marilyn Monroe.

Marilyn. Her posters sell in New York souvenir shops today, years and years after her death. What is it about Marilyn that has made her image endure? Why didn't Jayne Mansfield endure like that? Why didn't any other blonde reach the crowning place in the peroxide pantheon that Marilyn reached?

Let's review. Some blondes are all Summer Wheat, some all Apollo, some all Moon. Most blondes resolve a duality, have traits of an opposite blonde mixed into their characters: Summer Wheat and Apollo, Summer Wheat and Moon. Some blondes poke fun at blondeness, and try on Moon or Innocent as if they were trying on raincoats in spring.

But only one blonde was Summer Wheat and Moon and Innocent and Starlight and Champagne and . . . yes, even an Ironic Blonde, and that was Marilyn Monroe. She was the only blonde who was ever all blondes at once, and that's why we cannot forget her.

In any Marilyn Monroe performance—whether she's swathed in pink taffeta singing "Diamonds are a girl's best friend," or in sparkles singing "Happy Birthday" to John Kennedy, or flaunting her matador pants in *The Seven Year Itch*—Marilyn cycles through all the female blonde archetypal images possible. She plays them like a pianist plays runs—each character blends into the next, legato.

Adrienne Rich once called herself "an instrument in the shape of a woman." She was referring to the way she receives mental signals and turns them into poems. Well, Marilyn Monroe was also an instrument in the shape of a woman—she translated the pulsations of the mythic feminine into a moving image. She translated simultaneously and completely unconsciously. This was her glory and her tragedy.

Jung for Home Use

After four daughters, my father knew he was beaten and threw in the dynastic towel. He spent a good twenty years in a house with six women. Nevertheless, he smiles brightly whenever he sees one of us. This may be a defensive move.

Friends tell me that they regress to being fourteen years old every time they go back home. Back in the suburban house of his youth, even the paunchiest fifty-five-year-old insurance executive will start to bait his forty-five-year-old real estate broker sister while he stands at the refrigerator and chugs milk from the carton. Come in the old front door and you're at each other again—it's as if Rogaine and Viagra had not yet been invented.

In my family this tendency takes a different turn. As soon as my sisters and I gather about the familial dining table, a strange thing begins to happen. We morph. But not for us mere teenage baiting. No, we plunge right into the mythic prop closet and start pulling out breastplates and long braids. When we are apart, we are our lovely, adult, and individuated Selves. But when we are together, it's a Walkyrie convention.

It's true, none of us is particularly a wilting violet in everyday life. But when we meet, the blonde wattage spikes as we strap on our mythic masks and become the aspects of C. G. Jung's Great Mother archetype.

Throughout history, mankind has always had its finger on its own pulse. We have wondered, since the dawn of consciousness, just what we are and what we mean in the cosmos. And so we make up stories about what we mean and where we belong in the scheme of things.

Ancient civilizations projected their views of what they were into the great celestial unknown, or down into the depths of the earth, and worshiped gods and goddesses who dwelt somewhere *out there*.

Today, we no longer cast our belief "out there," and have turned, instead, to "in here." We have made ourselves our own cosmos, and look inward, rather than outward, or upward, for our explanations. Myth and religion once gave people their stories to live by. We need stories, too, to tell us what our context is, what the rules are, or what we can be. The kind of mind that would have been an Augustine, a Teresa, or an Aquinas in a past generation is now often a psychologist.

Today the discipline of psychology is the forum for thinkers who would understand humanity's actions, inactions, motives, and responses.

C. G. Jung believed that we all carry pictures in our heads that are composite reproductions of the feelings and the experiences of our ancestors. He thought all people are naturally inclined toward certain symbols, and that these symbols appear again and again in our dreams, in the things we make, and in how we live. He called these symbols "archetypes" because they recurred in all cultures and as images in most people's minds.

The way Jung saw it, everyone had a mother, everyone's mother had a mother, that mother had a mother, and so on and on, back down the line into the dark of prehistory. All these impressions of "motherness" are embedded in our brains—the multilayered image of what it means to be female is there when we are born, waiting, like an outline in a coloring book. It is an archetype. We spend our lives coloring in pictures that have already been outlined for us.

In our contemporary world, the image of the Great Mother is usually a blonde. You'll see her blonde in paintings, standing around blonde in a field of wheat, or casually holding a large basket filled with at least fifty pounds of fruit, blonde hair a-tumbling. And then there are the pictures of her clutching a baby to her breast, or holding the lifeless body of a soldier or a saint. In myth and painting and even on TV the golden blonde hair of the Great Mother image symbolizes her great value. She is good, she is fruitful, she is caring, and she is undefiled by wanton thoughts or deeds. Think of Florence Henderson on *The Brady Bunch*. No cheesy doings for Florence. She was not big on wanton thoughts or deeds, but very big on kids, dogs, and motivating Alice to make photogenic salad.

Jung knew that the mythic feminine had other sides, and that an image of what it was to be fully female couldn't just be all corn and babies. He saw a side that is angry and chaotic; a side that is sweet, lovable, and gentle; and a side that is cool and ambitious. In our time, we have a blonde for each of these sides. Our blondes represent all the facets of the Great Mother archetype.

"Fake it till you make it" is the inscription emblazoned on the heraldic crest of the blonde. Fake the power of the female sign and the power will come to you. Put on the mask of blonde and you can enter into a new personality, a personality that is stronger than your real Self, a persona that will take care of you during crises like nuclear war or Thanksgiving.

Take the case of Nadia, my eldest sister. After her formative Parisian years, she turned out to be an attractive, tall blonde-of-accomplishment prone to wearing Dana Buchman. After many kinds of blonde, she went with a nice Apollo Winter Sun shade, and it was for the best. In everyday life, Nadia works at a computer company, sees friends, has beaus, and kicks over the traces every once in a while by having pizza at her favorite dive. Add to this a lovely Victorian apartment and convenient storage unit, and you pretty much have Nadia.

But when we converge at the Las Gallinas dining room table, whether summoned by holiday or funeral, the first to morph into a Jungian archetype is Nadia. On goes the mask. Her shoulders start to go back, like the ears on an angry dog. Her usually graceful movements are replaced by a robotic efficiency. I often hear her muttering under her breath about the state of the china closet. That Apollo hair takes on a crisp texture not seen in her everyday life: She becomes all straight lines. Cool and assured, she is suddenly The Explainer of All Things and starts regaling you with a triumph in office politics when you are trying to mix salad dressing.

She would not normally do any of these things were she alone, or with her friends. But family will do things to you. You need power. You need a nice, comfy mask. In our family, Nadia wears the mask of Jung's Amazon, one of the faces of his archetypal feminine—all intellect, coolness, and ambition.

Lita is the next to put on her mask. Now, normally Lita is a Summer Wheat/Apollo cross, an upstanding member of the wine-country business community. I fully expect her to pledge the Kiwanis Club any day. Tall, curvaceous, and sexy, her wild, curly California Sun Blonde hair belies the cool Apollo MBA underneath. She and her daughter, Tati, live the small-town life, walking in the Fourth of July parade today, fighting the zoning battle tomorrow. Lita is a mom, she is a businesswoman, she is organized, she is tired.

But when Lita arrives for dinner at the familial home, she comes in the guise of the Angry Goddess, the archetypal feminine's aspect of wrath and vengeance. The four-by-four screeches to a halt in front of the house. In she stomps, looking like Athena after a showdown on the fields of Troy. Blonde hair windblown, blue eyes snapping, sporting togalike garb and work boots, she's late, she says, because some bozo on the road was going only seventy miles an hour. And by the way, here's the bread.

Nadia (counting the teaspoons) and Lita (furiously cutting up the bread) are not the only personalities mixing over the asparagus vinaigrette. My sister Anna, normally a tall, worked-out, minivan-jockeying Summer Wheat mother of two with long Nordic-blonde hair the texture of silk dupioni, quietly reaches for her mask and turns into the Princess aspect of the Great Mother, becoming a self-contained Innocent Blonde right before our eyes.

First she starts to radiate a golden glow. Then she gets this "Kumbaya" look on her face, which is not disturbed by her children using her as a jungle gym. She becomes love and kindness personified. This can be hard to take when one is trying to put on the soup.

Often, just when Lita and Tati are engaged in a comedy-team tussle over broccoli (Tati trying to convince her mother just to try some), and as Nadia is explaining computer drivers to a guest, Anna, one child on her lap, the other corralled with an arm, will decide to give one of those good old-fashioned Protestant blessings, the kind that go on for a while and feature abundance and goodwill toward men.

At these dinners I have trouble actually seeing my sisters in their masks because my mask is already on and it is difficult to look out of those tiny little eye holes.

And who am I, now that we've used up all the archetypal aspects of the Great Mother? Upon my return to the familial dinner table I embody another archetype found in Jung's portrait of the psyche: the Shadow. And the way I express my dark, bitter yearnings is by laughing at irritating things.

Now, in New York, I am not funny. I am serious, I am studious, I cry. People would say that I am a quiet woman, and that I keep to myself. I have gone out with men for years before they realized that I had a sense of humor. I remember my last boyfriend caught on because a stranger pointed it out to him on an airplane. "I just love your girlfriend," he said, "she'll laugh at anything."

So most people do not think me funny. But something happens when I cross the threshold at Las Gallinas. A little tension between the Angry Goddess and the Amazon? Zap goes my newfound sense of humor. I am arch. I am laconic. I am withering. They are all very tolerant and offer me Dubonnet when I start to channel Don Rickles. Inwardly, I seethe and plot their deaths. Outwardly, I'm funny.

Because of this irony problem, I spend a lot of time alone in the kitchen. It is pleasant there. Peaceful. Sometimes I spend the time thinking of ways to redeem myself and my image of the masculine from the forces of repression, hoping to bring to consciousness my capacity to trust love as something that combines "spirit" and "nature" in the best sense of the words. And sometimes I just stir chocolate sauce and play with the little whisk.

So there we are, Lita sparking, Nadia explaining, me seething, Anna blessing—all in all a vivified compendium of the female psyche. How my father takes all this, I will never know. I suppose he is quietly honing his anima, hoping for boys in the next life.

During these dinners, my mother sat, aware, perceiving, remembering, thinking, and feeling—the observing ego at the end of the table. With a nod of her head or a look your way across the china and flowers, she acknowledged the presence of an idea or a feeling and was the dark-haired gatekeeper of my family's consciousness.

Sometimes, after I had gotten off a crack that made her really laugh, her arm held across her waist as if to hold herself together, she would say, "Ta, you'd sacrifice your own mother for a joke!" It was her highest accolade. And now I see that she was right.

Old Blonde

I have a friend who gets a real chuckle out of what she perceives as Barbara Walters's continuing struggle to overcome neck cords. Anne announces Barbara's every alleged surgery, watching to see if she can pull off the improbable and return to the swanlike neck of her youth.

I don't know whether Barbara Walters has ever even thought about having neck surgery. But my friend's preoccupation intrigues me. Barbara is the original Power Blonde. Seriously Apollo. Why would a neck cord or two make any difference to her at this point in her career? She has climbed to an unshakable place in the human pyramid of blonde newscasters. The woman must have suction cups on her hands and knees. And yet cords matter. Because if she starts to look too old, she's had it. We Americans don't go for old blondes.

The fourth face of the mystical feminine, after the faces of sun and moon and innocence, is the face of the wise woman, the old crone. Crones aren't big in America. We like young. We fear old. And we particularly fear old women.

Now why is that? Why should old women be so unappreciated in our culture? I think maybe it's because we fear death, and we think that old women know too much. We fear age because age points to an ending, and we fear woman knowledge because a smart woman who's been around the block a few times can spot a pathetic fallacy at twenty paces. The idea that someone might see through our commercial smokescreen of aerosol deodorant to the bleak beyond is a horrendous thought for the Madison Avenue crowd. Or would be a horrendous thought if they ever let themselves think it.

Old Blondes, old-crone-hair-sticking-out-of-a-mole-in-the-chin, dried-up, post-menopausal blondes, give us the creeps. And that goes back to the idea of witches, an idea that isn't as dead and buried in the American consciousness as you might believe. The Salem witch trials were going along at the same time that the Age of Reason was flourishing in Europe, two hundred and fifty years ago. The two are not unconnected.

When the Catholics wanted to wipe out the remains of the pagan mother cults, which were scattered all over Europe in the twelfth and thirteenth centuries, they deemed the women who kept the rites "devil worshippers" and burned as many of them as they could. These women were a threat to the dominant order. If a woman was too powerful or owned too much land, a quick expedient was to declare her a witch and burn her.

Old women came to symbolize the forbidden knowledge of these mother cults, the remains of the cults of Demeter and of Epona and of Isis. A certain kind of smelly old woman came to be associated with the devil, who took the form of the goat she rode upon and with whom she was said to fornicate. Old women came to symbolize the repressed dark side of human experience, and everything that could not be admitted into the patriarchal construct that called itself Christianity was thrown upon her.

The goatish devil we see in old engravings of witches is a corruption of Pan, the satyr of Greek mythology. Half man, half goat, he represented a Dionysian insanity, bisexuality, and raw paganism that somehow just didn't whistle the right tune for the early Church. Everything insane, perverse, or morbid was thrown onto the "scapegoat" of the old woman who consorted with the devil. We're too grown up for this now. We just insist that witches don't exist.

Which brings us to bluehairs. Back in the drugstore, you'll find some blonde hair colors that are meant for only very old women. These are the pastel blondes. Many's the time I have sat in my hairdresser's chair at Irene's between an eighty-year-old with hair the color and texture of cotton candy and an eighty-nine-year-old with a pouf the color of the light violet haze of a November sunset.

If they can't be crones, where are our old ladies to go? How can they regain a scrap of their previous wise woman dignity and value? What other place—what other kind of blonde—can return to them a whisper of their former role of keeper of mysteries, of spiritual guide?

Our old ladies can't be carnal, scary, or witchlike. We don't allow it. They can't speak their physicality, their decay, their age. But they can align themselves with innocence. They can look like fairy godmothers, like tooth fairies, like sprites. We allow them to be fey, to regain innocence. And when they are very old, we allow them to go back to the state of children, to look like numinous angels with halo hair. We insist that they burn through their carnality, their sexuality, and stand on the precipice purified, as though by fire.

Fair Fame and the Goat Lady

The day that my editor had the idea for this book was the last day that my mother made it upstairs. I sat at the makeshift desk I had set up in the corner of my father's studio—fax machine, answering machine, a new, temporary second line—and I thought, I could write a book like that, and felt a huge rush, like the rush after someone pulls you back out of the way of an oncoming car.

That was when I heard the scrabbly sound, and walked down the hall to the top of the stairs, and saw my mother hauling herself up the banister, hand over hand, very slowly, very intently. She had the look that mountaineers have when they near the summit, out of oxygen, bent into the task, summoning all their strength for the next step.

Everything she had was going into that climb. She was concentrated on sending the message to walk from her cut-up brain to her feet.

A chirpy little nurse's aide was walking up the stairs slowly after her, not helping, of course, for this was physical therapy. She was saying spiritedly, "We're going to take a shower!" As if taking a shower were the most natural reason in the world to strain every muscle and every nervous connection to get up a staircase.

It is an interesting fad at this moment in medicine: If you are going to die, doctors like to exercise you until you actually do die, just in case you suddenly turn out to be the one in three thousand patients who goes into remission. They want you to be ready to strap on your dancing shoes, just in case.

This case was not the case with my mother. Shortly after she went into remission from breast cancer, they found a tumor in her lung. And after the tumor in her lung, they found a tumor in her brain the size of a baby's fist.

The choice was to not remove it, and die in two weeks. Or to remove it and probably die, oh, sometime, or perhaps not die at all, and strap on your dancing shoes. They removed it early on a crisp January morning. She lived thirteen more months.

After she had the surgery and was transferred to a rehabilitation hospital, we learned two things. The first was that they had cut out the part of her brain that tells you where you are. She knew she was in a room, but she didn't know what was outside the door to the room. Later, she knew she was in a room, but she didn't know where the room was, or that it was in the same house that she had lived in for thirty years.

The second thing we learned was that she was being visited every morning by the Goat Lady. The Goat Lady came every dawn. My mother could hear her shouts in the distance, and the crack of her whip over the miniature goats who pulled her cart. She was an old, wizened crone, with rather a goat-featured face, and her head was bound in a kerchief. She was not nice.

Just as it started to get light, my mother would hear the tapping of the little goat feet as they came along, straining and tentative, up the corridor of the hospital, and then she'd hear the crabby old Goat Lady coming along behind, riding on her cart, hallooing at her little charges.

Sometimes a goat would raise up on its little hind legs and put its forefeet on my mother's bed, and tell her, in plain English, not to worry about the nastiness of the Goat Lady, that she was that way to everybody, and then it would nimbly dash off before it was missed from the herd.

For the last thirteen months of her life, my mother lived in two very clearly separate worlds. She lived with us, in our house on Las Gallinas, in a relatively unaltered mental state. And she lived in a mythological world where the Goat Lady came at dawn, and people got lost in dark woods and then were found again or not found, and cats talked back. She rarely confused the two worlds, and out of an innate politeness often didn't mention it when a character came visiting our reality.

But sometimes she would say, "Do you see that cat by the sofa?" And I would say, "I don't see a cat in my reality, Mommy." And she would nod seriously, as if marking in her mind that the cat was living in Reality B, not Reality A. But generally she didn't mention it. She just didn't want us to worry that she'd lost her mind.

My mother went through an extreme split between her practical and her myth-making worlds. At the time when brain function failed her, her *mind* did not, and the myth-making function continued, making sense of things, providing a world for her, a world into which we could not truly follow.

We all live in these two separate worlds, the world of myth and the everyday world, and, though we seldom realize it, we spend much of our time combining them.

We are imbued with myth and storytelling. Our contemporary fairy tales, the ones we watch on TV, revolve around hospital emergencies, police action, galactic exploration. These settings show our desperate need to control the uncontrollable: Revive the patient, nab the suspect, map the universe.

The old stories of religion and myth seem dead to us, for we are living in the aftermath of the Enlightenment, in an age that has romanticized logic and science. We desperately hope that technology will save us from the part of ourselves that is unknowable. We have put all our eggs in the scientific basket, and now scientists are turning to us and saying, "You know, it's funny, looks like there are no hard-and-fast rules after all."

We spent three hundred years mapping where we are with a compass and a ruler, and now it turns out that, without warning, the ruler stretches every once in a while. But during those nice, orderly three hundred years, we systematically devalued the old stories, and now we really can't go back to them.

We have cut out the part of our brain that tells us where we are. We know we are in this life, but we don't know what is outside the door to this life. We know we are in a room, but we don't know where the room is, or whether the mental house that mankind has lived in for 30 million years is ours at all. The rise of science and the loss of myth—and now, the loss of the hard-and-fast rules that once were the bedrock of science—has left us nothing to believe in. We climb up the stairs through our lives, and society beams at us and says chirpy things but does not help us.

The ninth-century Vikings believed that there wasn't an afterlife unless you happened to be chosen to go to Valhalla after dying on the battlefield. But that was a one in three thousand chance, and few warriors strapped on their dancing shoes.

Their philosophy has been called "heroic resignation." You lived, you expected hardship, you didn't complain about it, you were a true friend and a brave foe. Your death was fated; you couldn't do anything about dying. But the way you were remembered by your friends, your kin, your leader—that was not fated. Were you a coward, or a hero? A scoundrel, or a leader? A strong woman, or a weak, gossiping woman? Did you die bravely, or did you die a cowardly, stupid death? How people remembered you was your only hope of immortality.

There is a verse in an Old Norse poem, chronicled in the Poetic Edda, dated around the ninth century, that says:

Cattle die   and kinsmen die
Thyself eke soon   wilt die;
but fair fame   will fade never,
I ween,   for him who wins it.

And that's what blondes believe. They choose to look bigger than they are: more innocent, stronger, prettier, sexier, tougher, cooler, or more obvious. They attempt to be more goddesslike, more known, because they want to be remembered. They want to live heroic lives. They blend their Reality A with their Reality B. They pull the myth of themselves into their real life of kids and divorce and loneliness, and find a happiness in the belief that they will be remembered as waiflike, or sexy, or beautiful. They strive to endure.

When my mother finally made it up the stairs, had the shower, and was resting in an armchair in her bedroom, I told her about the idea for a blonde book. I said my editor thought I should write about why women go blonde. She looked at me, her clear eyes bright in her tired face, and said, "Do you think you can write it?" I said, "Yes, I can write it." And she said, "Write it, then."

Touchstone Reading Group Guide

Blonde Like Me

Discussion Questions

1. *Blonde Like Me* appears to be a book about hair color. But it is really a book about identity. What are we trying to tell the world when we go blonde? Why do so many women choose to go blonde? What are you trying to tell the world when you cut, curl, perm, color, or grow your hair?

2. Fashion is a system of signs. We signal what we are thinking of ourselves and others by what we wear. Quick takes: say what high heels mean, what black leather means, what white lace means, what flat shoes mean. Why do these articles of clothing mean anything? Ask each person in the room to describe what she or he is wearing. Do you all agree? Is that person sending the signals that he wants to send? Is she aware of what she is saying with her clothes?

3. Changing your hair, wearing makeup, even picking out certain kinds of clothing can be a form of self-expression, but can also be a kind of mask. Think about some of the masks you have worn. Did you put them on voluntarily? Were you trying to conform to a cultural standard? Were you trying to avoid something unpleasant?

4. If a woman is trying to tell the world something through her hair color, makeup (or lack of it), and clothing, what might she also be trying to tell herself? Can changing the outer you also change the inner you? If the world treats you differently, do you become . . . different?

5. On a lighter note, Natalia Ilyin points out that there are different kinds of blondes as well as subsets of those blondes. The possibilities here are endless. What are the distinguishing features of an East-Side-of-Manhattan blonde? A Connecticut blonde? A Texas blonde? A corn-fed Midwest blonde? A Santa Barbara blonde? How are they different? Think of the blondes you know and start making up classifications for them. Then think about why you are classifying them that way!

Discover more reading group guides online!

Browse our complete list of guides and download them for free at **www.SimonSays.com/reading_guides.html**